Further Praise for *The Art of Governing Coherently*

"This book aims to help boards stay aligned to the true meaning of governance and holds them accountable for leadership and change management. Boards can become distracted by all the shiny aspects of operations, but this book confirms why staying true to coherent governance lends itself to better results."

—*Deborah Hendrix, former president, Harrison School District 2 Board of Education, Colorado Springs, Colorado; executive director, Parents Challenge*

"I couldn't be more clear of my authority, boundaries, limitations, and expectations, while our board has never felt so informed and empowered to improve student learning. This has truly provided us a roadmap to success."

—*John Steach, superintendent, Evergreen, Washington, School District*

"Practical, simple and direct advice is coupled with concise formats that successfully support the Board and CEO in this quality governance model."

—*Brad Mayne, CVE, International Association of Venue Managers, Dallas, Texas*

"If you are on a school board and things are not going well. Or . . . something is not right and you don't know enough to know what is wrong. Or . . . you just want to do it the right way. Check out this book and then call them!"

—*Richard Clapp, member, Palm Springs Unified School District, California*

The Art of Governing Coherently

Mastering the Implementation of Coherent Governance® and Policy Governance®

Linda J. Dawson and Randy Quinn

ROWMAN & LITTLEFIELD
Lanham • Boulder • New York • London

Published by Rowman & Littlefield
A wholly owned subsidiary of The Rowman & Littlefield Publishing Group, Inc.
4501 Forbes Boulevard, Suite 200, Lanham, Maryland 20706
www.rowman.com

6 Tinworth Street, London SE11 5AL

Copyright © 2019 by Linda J. Dawson and Randy Quinn

All rights reserved. No part of this book may be reproduced in any form or by any electronic or mechanical means, including information storage and retrieval systems, without written permission from the publisher, except by a reviewer who may quote passages in a review.

British Library Cataloguing in Publication Information Available

Library of Congress Cataloging-in-Publication Data Available

ISBN 978-1-4758-4622-5 (cloth : alk. paper)
ISBN 978-1-4758-4623-2 (pbk. : alk. paper)
ISBN 978-1-4758-4624-9 (electronic)

Contents

Foreword		vii
Preface		xi
Acknowledgments		xv
1	A Word about Governing Models	1
2	Rolling Out Your Model	7
3	Monitoring Governance Culture and Board-CEO Relations Policies	17
4	Monitoring Operational Expectations Policies	27
5	Monitoring Results Policies	57
6	Evaluating the CEO in This New Governing Environment	73
7	Engagement	87
8	The Board's Annual Work Plan	107
9	The Board's New Meeting Agenda	113
10	Change: It's a Leadership Conundrum	123
11	Now What?	131
Appendix A: Monitoring Operational Expectations Policies for Compliance		139

Appendix B: Monitoring Operational Expectations Policies
for Compliance — 149

Appendix C: Monitoring Results for Reasonable Progress — 157

Appendix D: Results Monitoring Report — 161

Appendix E: Engagement with Stakeholders — 169

Appendix F: Engagement Plan to Further Define Results — 173

Appendix G: Board Listening Campaign — 177

Appendix H: Agendas for Good Governance — 181

Appendix I: Typical Agenda Outline for Public Board — 183

Glossary — 185

About the Authors — 187

Foreword

In 1999, Alberta's learning minister, Dr. Lyle Oberg, made the extraordinary decision to dismiss the entire elected board of trustees of the Calgary Board of Education (CBE). The minister concluded that personal and political differences among the trustees had rendered the board dysfunctional. He was aware of the drastic consequences of the action he was taking, but he was convinced that the board had lost its ability to focus on its role as the governing entity of the school system. After trying to work with the board, he dismissed the trustees and called a by-election to elect a new board.

When I was elected in 1999 to the new Calgary Board of Education as a school board trustee, I was fueled by my desire to make a difference for my community and by my firm belief that a strong public education system is fundamental to a strong democratic society. I was certainly aware of the damage the dismissal of the previous board had done to the school system that I now wished to join. I headed into my role as a new school board member with very little understanding of the system I was joining or the place of school board members within it. I knew the organization I was joining had had its struggles, but I soon learned that I had stepped into a disorderly system where, despite several previous efforts to improve its governance quality, success had been elusive.

The seven of us on the board agreed that we needed a better governance system to support our work. The board needed to own its work and play its proper role in governing the school system. Through diligent research and previous experiences, we recognized that we needed to operate through policy, and we were drawn to Policy Governance as a system within which to operate.

Fortunately, we found Dr. Randy Quinn and Linda Dawson and made a commitment to engage them to coach us into the practice of Policy Governance.

They supported the board by helping us focus on the organization's purpose and develop clear governing policies. From these new policies flowed the organizational goals and the means to effectively measure results. They also helped us grapple with the board's critical relationship with the CEO and the need to genuinely connect with the owners of the organization. Later, when Linda and Randy developed their Coherent Governance model, our board saw the wisdom of converting to it, which became CBE's governance operating system.

From the abyss of complete elimination of the board of trustees in 1999, because of its failure to provide adequate leadership for the CBE, came a major transformation. In 2007, that same board that had lost its existence became the overall winner of the Conference Board of Canada/Spencer Stuart National Award in Governance. The board also won the national award that same year in the public-sector category. There were several fundamental reasons for this dramatic turnaround in the board's performance, but at the root of it all was the board's reliance on Coherent Governance, and the implementation protocols presented in this book, to enable it to lead CBE in an organized and effective way.

Linda and Randy are unafraid to challenge board members with words like "discipline" and "focus." And because of their depth of experience, they can support boards with tools that use discipline and focus to achieve results.

Several other key words find their way into any discussion of quality governance. "Commitment" is one of those words—commitment to the process, to effective monitoring, and to the board's own consistent performance.

"Maturity" pops up on a regular basis—why do board members sometimes behave in childlike ways when given the authority to make crucial decisions on behalf of an organization?

"Reasonable" is another word that factors strongly into Coherent Governance. Reasonable is sometimes a high bar for humans to reach, but we should try! Randy and Linda not only define and use these words; they model them.

"Clarity" is a key word that resonates throughout this book—it is a personal favorite of mine. Board members need to understand their roles within the organization—what they should and should not do, which decisions belong to the board and which to the CEO and administration. Success of the organization is a shared goal, but the form of participation in pursuit of that success is what differentiates a board from its administration. Terms and roles must be clear and mutually understood. There is nothing worse than having a conversation and realizing that two people are using the same word very differently—hard to address during a debate in a board meeting!

Board members also must be clear about the purpose and function of the board, as opposed to members' individual thoughts, opinions, and actions. This is very often where boards can go sideways as individuals try to press their own issues or want to be the star of the show. In Coherent Governance, the board is the star of the show.

The recommendations and ideas presented in this book are not purely theoretical concepts. The processes and strategies have been tested over time with hundreds of organizations. Reading this book reminded me of the many errors and pitfalls encountered by boards on which I have served throughout the years. I would read a section and say to myself, "Yes, we did that"; or "Oops! Forgot about that one"; or "Grr, I remember having to deal with that behavior from a fellow board member."

I also was reminded of the many successes I have witnessed and participated in as a board member, and of the power of human beings coming together with a common purpose and focus. It is a good reminder that boards are made up of people. That reality can be extremely challenging, but it can also be quite spectacular.

Randy and Linda, through Coherent Governance, have provided a strong governance system, templates, and tools. They also have reinforced what we all knew already: Organizational change is not easy, people are not easy, and discipline (there's that word again!) is not easy. Simply adopting Coherent Governance will not cause an organization to be successful. If a board commits to the application of the processes recommended in this book, it has a good chance for success—a resilient, tested system with plenty of support for implementation.

I wish you success as you work to implement Coherent Governance or Policy Governance for the first time, or as you continue to improve the governance model chosen by your board to lead your organization. Reading this book will surely be helpful in generating new ideas about implementation strategies that can breathe life into the abstract model. Plunging in with enthusiasm will change your organization for the better and enhance your governance capacity. It will help your board improve the services and benefits for the people whom your organization serves—and isn't that why boards exist?

> Pat Cochrane, Former Chair
> Calgary Board of Education Board of Trustees
> Calgary, Alberta, Canada

Preface

The fact that you are reading this book likely indicates that your board has adopted either Coherent Governance or Policy Governance, and now is concerned with properly implementing the model. Or it could mean that your board has made an attempt at implementation, and it is frustrated with the challenge to do it "correctly."

We know how you feel.

Both Coherent Governance® and Policy Governance® are extraordinary tools to help boards govern well, both based on sound principles and commonsense logic. But only if a governing model is implemented in a meaningful way can it deliver on its promise of good governance. Otherwise, it can be more frustrating than helpful. It actually can become an impediment rather than a useful tool for good governance.

Without some type of road map that indicates what to do, when, and how, proper implementation can be a daunting challenge for boards unaccustomed to the discipline of doing their own work and using such a well-defined system. Boards are required to do things they have never done, and the things they have done they must do in sometimes dramatically different ways. New and different skills are required, and higher levels of personal and group discipline are necessary—if the system is to provide the degree of added value the board envisioned when its journey toward good governance began.

But proper implementation doesn't have to be a death-defying experience. There are some very sensible, easily accomplished strategies that both boards and their CEOs can follow to take their model from the abstract to the real, and make it work as a well-oiled machine.

We refer to this as the "putting it on the ground and making it roll" stage. It is the fun part of transitioning from a board's having no defined way to get its work done to a logical, planned process for leading the organization for which the board is responsible, at an unprecedented level of effectiveness.

This book is a "how to" implementation training manual for boards that have adopted either Coherent Governance or Policy Governance. Although we will offer a very brief overview of the two models in Chapter 1, it is assumed that the reader has some working knowledge of one or both of the models, and is concerned more with proper implementation than with understanding the model.

For readers who do not have some working knowledge of either of the models, we recommend first reading our book *Good Governance Is a Choice*, which will set a base for a greater understanding of the procedures and strategies recommended in this book.

Throughout this book, we use the terminology of Coherent Governance rather than Policy Governance. For readers who are more familiar with Policy Governance terms, the translation from Policy Governance to Coherent Governance should be an easy one. The labels used for the four quadrants of policy are presented in Exhibit 1.1 in Chapter 1.

Readers will note that many of the examples and references used throughout this book come from the world of school boards and public education. That is a deliberate choice for two very good reasons. Our dominant client base is public school boards, and thus our supply of good examples is greater from that field.

But equally important in our decision to use school board examples is our realization that everyone is familiar with public schools. All of us are or have been affiliated with them as students, parents of students, or if nothing else, a part of their "ownership," since we all pay taxes for their support. Public education may be one of the most challenging of all environments in which to implement a dramatically different governing model. Our belief is that if it can be done here, it can be done anywhere.

As we say numerous times in the following pages, there is no single way to implement either Coherent Governance or Policy Governance. Both models are elegant in their simplicity, but both can be challenging to actually use and practice faithfully.

The implementation strategies recommended in this book will work; we have tried them all, and we know them to be effective. Other processes also may work, but we don't know that. Our best recommendation for boards and CEOs new to the practice of one of these models is to establish implementation strategies based on known and established processes, then deviate later if there is reason to do so. Bad habits can take root very quickly, and they are difficult to change once begun.

Changing board and organizational cultures, agendas, internal reporting processes, protocols, and literally almost everything else isn't easy. But faithful implementation, we believe, positions the board to provide leadership in ways that it never before has experienced and aligns the entire organization to achieve its vision and Results. Our objective is to make a difficult job as manageable and as user-friendly as possible.

Acknowledgments

We express our deep admiration of and appreciation to our many clients whose work is the foundation for this book. Many of them eagerly have participated in some trial-and-error ventures that ultimately established workable processes and systems that this book now shares. Their perseverance and determination to succeed, sometimes against great odds, is inspirational.

We especially thank those clients who have proven the viability of the implementation processes described in this book and have contributed much of the work shared in this book as examples. Some of these examples are attributed directly to those boards and organizations that created them, while others are left unidentified, usually for obvious reasons. Some examples are not attributed due to the interval between their creation and this book's publication, and the wholesale changes in personnel during the intervening years.

We extend our sincere gratitude to our client boards, CEOs, and organizations. We appreciate them not only for the opportunities they have given us to coach them in their governance work, but also for their acceptance of the challenge to elevate their own performance, as demonstrated by the quality work they have produced and their willingness to allow us to share it with readers throughout the world.

Chapter One

A Word about Governing Models

Models are just that: models. They provide a framework for the board to do its job, and to express clear expectations for organizational performance. We frequently refer to governing models as operating systems for boards. They serve the same function as computer operating systems in that they help organize processes and data to enable a logical and well-ordered outcome. Governing models are not ends to themselves, but rather, they are a means to a much larger and more important end: good governance. They provide a systematic framework intended to position boards to organize their work and lead their organizations in some coherent fashion.

On occasion, consultants and others refer to a "traditional" governing model. Actually, for most boards, a traditional governing model isn't a model at all; it is the *absence* of a model. Too often and for far too many boards, governance is a cobbled-together mix of practices based on tradition. There usually is no rhyme or reason why boards do what they do, other than that they have always done things that way. And their processes typically reflect the personalities and experiences of members currently serving on the board, along with those of the CEO.

In our experience, there are only two true, complete governing models, our own Coherent Governance and John Carver's Policy Governance. Some boards and consultants use features of both models, and attach other names to the resulting hybrid.

In order to qualify as a full-form governance model, we believe the system must be policy-based; must cover the full range of board responsibilities; must have form and structure sufficient to drive complete organizational alignment; must be designed to focus both board and staff on organizational results; and must eliminate role confusion by establishing clear lines of delegated authority and strict accountability.

Both Policy Governance and Coherent Governance have form and structure that hold the separate parts together in a coherent whole. Both models are policy-based systems driven by values, enabling boards to effectively lead the organizations for which they are responsible and make decisions that are theirs to make at the policy level.

Both models feature a small number of policies, usually not more than thirty or so. The policies are grouped into four quadrants, each serving a distinct purpose.

The real value of using either Coherent Governance or Policy Governance is that both models are based on principles experts long have recognized as being characteristics of effective boards. While both models may require board behaviors that are very different from the customary behaviors of many boards, they are very consonant with the behaviors usually *expected* of all boards. Coherent Governance and Policy Governance are, in the truest sense, vehicles to enable boards to actually perform the way boards are intended to perform.

Some boards and board members resist the idea of adopting anything that has to do with a "model" or any organized governance system. They rebel against any structure they think may limit their individual freedoms, might be perceived as inconsistent with the local culture, or may inhibit their ability to provide off-the-cuff direction to the organization.

For a board to attempt to govern effectively with no defined operating system is akin to trying to play a team sport without a set of rules or a game plan. On occasion, it may work. But more often than not, confusion, disappointment, and frustration are the results for both the board and its staff, rather than organizational progress.

Sometimes organizational success may be achieved in spite of the board, rather than because of it. But typically, organizational performance will be no better than board performance.

In most organizations, good governance doesn't exist unless the board deliberately creates it. A coherent governing model, based on fundamental principles and values, can allow the board to build something greater than itself, enabling members to leave a legacy of visionary leadership for those members and staff leaders who follow.

We always caution boards that seem intellectually drawn to a governing model to recognize that the mere adoption of a new set of policies, or even the model itself, does not guarantee better governance. Good governance requires the practice of extraordinary discipline and commitment to the underlying principles of the model, or inevitably the time, effort, and money that went into developing the system will be wasted.

No governing system is any better than the people who are trying to implement it. This, more than any other factor, led us to write this book as a means to help boards develop and practice operational procedures and systems that will breathe life into their governing model and allow it to work for the board.

The following paragraphs very briefly describe the two models that are the focus of this book: our own Coherent Governance, and John Carver's Policy Governance. No attempt is made in this book to offer full descriptions of either model. Readers are expected to have a preexisting working knowledge of one or both models. For those who do not, we suggest Carver's *Boards That Make a Difference* as a source for Policy Governance information, and our own *Good Governance Is a Choice* for more information about Coherent Governance.

POLICY GOVERNANCE

Policy Governance is a registered service mark of Dr. John Carver. The ® symbol will not be used each time the words "Policy Governance" appear in this book, but readers are advised that the words refer to the governing model created and owned by Carver. Carver introduced his Policy Governance model to the world in the 1980s with the publication of his first book, *Boards That Make a Difference*. Policy Governance is based upon a set of traditional principles that people long have recognized as standards that good boards strive to practice. Carver recognized the difficulty that boards have in actually putting those principles into practice, and he created his model to enable boards to more effectively lead, direct, inspire, and control organizations through carefully crafted policy statements based on the principles.

The Policy Governance board sets policy and rigorously monitors organizational performance for both operations and outcomes. The policies are grouped into four categories:

Ends: Ends policies define organizational products and outcomes for specified beneficiaries. They clearly state the "bottom line" the organization is expected to achieve over time: What benefit? For whom? At what cost?
Executive Limitations: EL policies set clear limits and controls on operational decisions that the board would find unacceptable. They define the boundaries within which the CEO and staff may operate. All EL policies are stated prohibitively, and they serve to limit CEO authority and choices in pursuit of the Ends.
Governance Process: GP policies define the board's own work and how it will be carried out. They clearly state the expectations the board has for itself, for the chair, for individual members, and for collective board behavior, including behavior at board meetings and for any board committees.

Governance-Management Connection: These policies define the specific delegation of authority to the CEO, a process and timeline for CEO evaluation, and accountability of the CEO.

Since its creation, Policy Governance has been recognized universally as a sound model based on solid theory. It offers a logical process for boards to govern well, and to remove themselves from the day-to-day operational matters that too frequently consume board members' time and attention. At the same time, the model allows the board to control, through policy, the extent of authority delegated to the CEO and staff, and to monitor actual organizational performance to assure complete accountability.

COHERENT GOVERNANCE

Coherent Governance is our own governance design, influenced by John Carver's work. It is a variation of Policy Governance, resulting from our own work with clients whose actual needs seemed to require more than modest changes to existing models. The ® symbol will not be used each time the words "Coherent Governance" appear in this book, but readers are advised that the words refer to the governing model created and owned by AGI: Aspen Group International, LLC.

In particular, the modifications are geared to meet the specific conditions that exist in many public and nonprofit organizations, especially in the field of public education and other environments with elected board members. The changes are intended to address the full range of operational issues and concerns such boards face.

The Coherent Governance model is built around four different but interrelated types of policies, each serving a very distinct purpose:

Results: Results policies describe the outcomes the organization is expected to achieve for the specific clients or customers it serves. Results policies are the performance targets for the CEO and the organization, and they form the basis for judging the success of both based on the judgment of reasonable progress toward achieving targets.

Operational Expectations: Most boards want to remove themselves from preoccupation with the day-to-day operations of the organization. Yet they have concerns about those operational matters that they must express in order to represent and serve the interests of the board's "owners," those on whose behalf the board does its work. The range of concerns addressed by OE policies is much broader than is acceptable in PG, but our conviction is that the board cannot confidently delegate decision-making without first stating its concerns about every element of operational performance.

OE policies allow the board either to direct that certain conditions exist or actions occur, or to prohibit those conditions and actions the board would find unacceptable. Each OE policy is clearly and unambiguously stated, and each has two components: one stated positively ("do this"), the other negatively ("don't do this").

The CEO is required to comply with the board's stated values about operational conditions and actions. OE policies allow the board to control operational decisions without the role-confusing ritual of approving CEO recommendations, which undermines clear accountability.

The Coherent Governance board rigorously monitors organizational *compliance* (achieving the nonnegotiable "gold standard" of operations) with its Operational Expectations policies and *reasonable progress* toward the achievement of its Results policies.

Board-CEO Relations: BCR policies define the degree of authority delegated by the board to the CEO, and also outline the process for CEO evaluation. Essentially, the performance of the CEO and the performance of the organization are the same: If the organization succeeds in operating according to the board's stated values, and if it produces the outcomes specified by the board in policy, the CEO has succeeded, and the annual evaluation will reflect that success. (Let us note here that for the purposes of consistency, we will use the term *CEO* to include the titles of the executive heads of any organization, be that executive director, superintendent, chief superintendent, and in some cases, even president.)

Governance Culture: All boards have cultures. In traditional governing environments, we aren't quite sure what caused them to be what they are. In Coherent Governance, the board deliberately and carefully crafts a set of policies that, in sum, establishes a culture for good governance. Separate policies establish standards for how the board performs its work, including policies that define the board's job, its purpose, and its accountability.

Both Coherent Governance and Policy Governance establish standards of performance for everything, from the boardroom to the boiler room.

- The Governance Culture/Governance Process policies set the standards for the board's own performance.
- The Board-CEO Relationship/Governance-Management Connection policies set standards for how the board will interact with the CEO, defining what organizational success is and how it will be monitored.

- The Operational Expectations/Executive Limitations policies establish operational standards for the entire organization.
- The Results/Ends policies define the standard for organizational outcomes, specifically the value promised to those served by the organization.

In sum, then, both Coherent Governance and Policy Governance are complete systems enabling governing boards to do their work in a logical way that drives organizational response and alignment. Both models require commitment and discipline by the board, support and serious attention by the CEO and staff, and patience by all while new skills are learned and new processes are developed. Exhibit 1.1 identifies the nomenclature for both models:

Exhibit 1.1. Policy Titles in CG and PG

Policy Quadrant	Coherent Governance	Policy Governance
One	GC: Governance Culture	GP: Governance Process
Two	BCR: Board/CEO Relationship	GMC: Governance Management Connection
Three	OE: Operational Expectations	EL: Executive Limitations
Four	R: Results	E: Ends

The remainder of this book is focused on the specific strategies and processes that we recommend boards and CEOs consider as the model is implemented, beginning with initial steps to announce the board's new way of doing business, then progressing through all the essential components of effective implementation. Chapter 2 begins that journey with suggestions for rolling out the model to owners and both internal and external groups that have an interest in the work of the board.

Chapter Two

Rolling Out Your Model

You have done something important. You have laid the foundation for implementing a complete new governing system featuring very few, but clear policies calling for systemic and systematic organizational alignment to achieve your expectations. You have:

- Made a commitment to forge stronger relationships with the owners you represent and serve, seeking to ensure that their desired results for the clients served by your organization are achieved;
- Made a commitment to elevate your focus to allow the board to spend the bulk of its time dealing with what really matters: the benefits your clients are entitled to receive as a result of your efforts;
- Agreed to hold your CEO—and therefore the entire staff—accountable for achieving Results;
- Established clear performance expectations for your CEO, with regular monitoring processes built in; and
- Committed to govern the organization with great discipline from the *policy* level.

Now, how and when do you present this new focus and these commitments to the people who need to know? How can you build understanding of and support for this bold new venture? How do you explain to key staff how this adoption of a new governing model will affect them and their jobs?

Chapter Two

GETTING STARTED

This is our best advice, with some exceptions we will discuss later: Simply adopt the policies and start your journey. Begin your new work, allowing your internal operating processes and the texture of your board meetings themselves to gradually educate those who need to know what you have done, at least those outside the organization. People assume that the board has some means for doing its work, so usually there is little need for them to understand the intricacies of what those processes are. For people inside the organization, that may not always be the case, as we will discuss later.

Begin the journey by taking action to adopt the policies with a formal motion, similar to the following:

> Over the past ___ months, the board deliberatively and thoughtfully has created a new set of governing policies that will allow us to lead this organization in a much more powerful and accountable way. All members have participated in this venture. We have refined our values-driven policies to the point that we are ready to adopt and begin this exciting journey toward aligned and improved organizational performance, beginning in the boardroom and extending to every worksite.
>
> Therefore, Mr./Madam President, I move that the board adopt our completed set of governing policies, and appropriately refer all of our current operational policies to the CEO for his/her use in the day-to-day operation of the organization.

Notice that the motion has two significant parts:

- *Part one* moves that the board adopt its new policies.
- *Part two* moves that all current policies be referred to the CEO. This is important, especially if yours is a public board, because many or most of your old policies likely are based on some state or federal mandate and therefore they must be retained in some fashion. We recommend renaming these "Operational Policies," and making them the property of the CEO. They should retain the "policy" designation, since in many instances they are policies required by some superior authority.

  By designating these as "Operational Policies," they clearly are separated from the board's new "Governing Policies," and now are the responsibility of the CEO for the routine operation of the organization. It is at the CEO's level of operations that they have the most import anyway. In our experience, most of them are much too detailed, prescriptive, and regulatory for effective governance use.

  Some may question whether the board is taking an undue risk by referring its old policies to the CEO. *It is not*. OE-1 requires the CEO to comply with the law, and thus the CEO has no discretion to circumvent any current or future provisions of those policies that are legally required. Some boards want to know about changes made to the operational policies by the CEO. We see no basic problem with the CEO's providing that kind of information to the board as long as it is purely an exchange of information and not being presented to the board for approval.

After the board's approval of its new governing policies, let's consider some rollout strategies to position the board for success.

HITTING THE MARK...
WITHOUT CREATING A TARGET

We prefer and recommend a very low-key strategy to begin the board's work using the new governance system. However, if the board feels compelled to make some public announcement about the new system, we strongly encourage the board to *completely avoid the use of a label*. Labeling your efforts can create a highly convenient target. If your owners, stakeholders, and staff think they have another new trend to survive, it will be easy for them to take potshots at everything. And if a visible label is attached ("Coherent Governance"), sooner or later, it will become "the reason" for whatever future problems the organization encounters.

Instead, focus on the board's commitment to realign its own performance. Something like the following may be a reasonable statement to make:

> The board has allowed itself to become overly involved in issues related to day-to-day operations that have prevented us from focusing on organizational results. Members have committed to elevate our primary focus to the results the organization should achieve for the people we serve, and to remove ourselves from preoccupation with routine management operations. The board has adopted a new set of governing policies to enable it to better lead this organization. The CEO will execute his/her job without interference from the board, but with rigorous accountability and regular reporting of organizational performance and compliance with the board's policies.

Notice that the label "Coherent Governance" or "Policy Governance" is never used. The board has adopted new *governance policies*. Avoidance of labels is a good practice to observe.

Never fail to underscore this emphasis on clear accountability for delegated decisions. People who do not understand the governing model may choose to criticize the board for having given too much authority to the CEO. Such assumptions are completely false, of course, but people, especially those who do not understand the offsetting accountability inherent to Coherent Governance, tend to focus more on delegation than on accountability.

Another explanation of your enhanced board role that may apply (this is for a school board, but it may be modified for use by any organization) could sound like this:

> We have heard from our public that academic performance in the district must improve. To model and lead that improvement, we as a board are committed to our own self-improvement through a dedicated focus on student success. In the future, discussions about student achievement throughout the district will dominate our agendas. We actively will engage all segments of our community in this ongoing challenge by providing an instructional program to ensure that our students are individually challenged and meet or exceed the highest and most rigorous standards.

Big statements. Big commitment. But now is not the time to portray an image that you are doing something radical that would cause a backlash of concern. You are simply going to do the job you were elected or appointed to do: operate as a board exercising prudence and wisdom through your simple, clear policies to set the direction for your organization. And you are going to release the CEO and staff to do their jobs, yet hold them responsible for making results happen.

Another step in the process we have found to be effective, especially for boards that meet in public, is this: As the board formally adopts its new system, consider asking each board member, as well as the CEO, to speak to the reason they support this change and the improvements they hope for as this process unfolds. It is powerful to see and hear a unified board/CEO team embracing this journey together. It can help to mitigate any negativity from outside the board family in case people are motivated to instigate friction by creating factions.

INFORMING STAFF

Staff members, at least at the senior level, must be brought into the loop. After all, if the board's new vision for the organization never leaves the boardroom, not much will change within the organization. Alignment from the boardroom throughout the operational side of the organization is necessary for anything meaningful to occur, and that cannot happen without key staff members understanding and supporting the operational changes that will be driven by the board's work and their role in the evolution.

Staff members likely will know that the board has been working on new policies and a new governance process. For them, there is a "FUD" factor (*Fear, Uncertainty, and Doubt*) at work. What will happen to them? How will this new board focus change their lives? Their position could swing negatively against accepting and supporting the board's new venture, unless deliberate steps are taken to ensure a full understanding of what the board has done and why.

The question is, who should bring staff members into the loop? The governing policies provide that all staff members report to the CEO, and the CEO is the board's only employee. Does this mean that the board cannot interface with any staff to explain the model and the important role the board depends on staff to play in advancing the organization?

Strict interpretation of the model could suggest that to be the case. However, common sense must come into play here. The culture, size, and complexity of the organization itself must be considered. The only hard and fast rule we recommend is that the board and the CEO jointly decide how much board face time might be constructive in presenting this new venture to staff and how much of that burden the CEO wants to assume without the board's involvement.

We have worked with organizations in which the task was accomplished quite effectively with the board playing no role. In others, the CEO chose to invite the board or a board representative to interface directly with senior staff for extensive give-and-take, and this, too, worked very well. We emphasize that if the board and CEO agree that there is a constructive role for the board to play in informing staff, the task for the board is to *inform,* not to direct the work of staff.

However the work is organized, we recommend that the void be filled quickly with information and positive statements. The CEO should determine when, where, and how to ensure that top administrative staff fully understand all they need to know about the board's governing work, the Results to be achieved, the standards for operation with which they must comply, and how the work of staff may be affected.

If the board meets with senior administrative staff members directly, it should emphasize that the board respects their professionalism, experience, and expertise, *and that the board recognizes its job to be different from theirs.* The model releases them to do their work, with the board's support, as the CEO and staff align organizational processes with the board's expectations for Results and for operational decision-making.

Senior administrative staff members must grasp the concept that this is organization-wide and strategic alignment initiated and modeled by the governing board. The board will direct and evaluate only the CEO, and only through policy. In turn, all staff members will be directed and evaluated by the CEO based upon their contribution to achieving reasonable progress on Results and their faithful compliance with the operational policies.

A caution: Staff must have full and accurate information about what the board is doing, without the "reform of the month" flavor. Effective implementation of systems and processes can take months or even years to fully achieve. Staff need to understand that they will not outlive the board's commitment to move the organization in a new direction.

If the board meets with staff below senior administration level, it should be with the understanding that the purpose is to ensure full knowledge of what the board has done and how it will affect them, and *not* to build direct relationships around the CEO. Any such meetings should be acceptable with the CEO, who should be a part of the discussions.

STAFF AS AMBASSADORS

Staff members are known to be credible, go-to sources for information about the organization. Indeed, research tells us that the owners usually find the staff to be more credible than board members or the CEO. In schools, parents accept their child's teacher's opinion before all others. Families of elders in support care find the elders themselves to be the first line of information. The board's challenge is to ensure that key staff understand the board's focus and direction and are prepared to advocate for it within the universe of which they are a part.

Below are examples of how two clients chose to ensure initial staff understanding of the board's work.

EXAMPLE A

Keiro Northwest is a nonprofit, community-based elder care system serving Asian seniors across the community in Seattle, Washington. The board and CEO recognized that staff members, who also are intimately tied to the small and close-knit community, would be opinion leaders for family members, clients, and community members who would begin to see a change and wonder how this work was benefiting the organization's elder clients.

The rollout for Keiro Northwest became a three-step process. First, before work began with the board, at the request of the board and CEO, we met with senior staff to assure that they understood where the project would lead in terms of board focus and how it ultimately would affect staff work.

Second, once the policies were adopted and the board agendas and other board work began to change, we met with all senior staff members for a second overview of Coherent Governance and to respond to any questions or concerns they had based on the specific policy product the board had produced.

Finally, we conducted a meeting between senior staff and board for the purpose of building a stronger bridge of mutual understanding and a relationship that would serve them as they work together to meet their owners' and clients' needs. The board wanted to have an honest give-and-take session with staff about their concerns and hopes.

EXAMPLE B

After a large school board in Texas adopted a new governance model several years ago, it challenged the superintendent to ensure that his staff of more than 11,000 employees, including 450 administrators at 120 school sites, understood the board's new emphasis and how it would affect their jobs. It was a Herculean task that called for a plan for systemic communication and commitment.

Below are two documents that illustrate the superintendent's two-step approach to presenting the board's work to internal staff at all levels. This effort ensured that all staff members knew what this new venture was before the board began a series of linkages throughout the community to build support for the Results.

Office of the CEO
ACTION REQUIRED
Memorandum

To: Principals
From: CEO
Subject: Professional Development Regarding the Board's Governance Model
Date: November 7

As part of the District's transition to a new governance model, we need to conduct an awareness initiative over the next three months.

It is my expectation that you will share this information with your campus staff, campus advisory councils, and PTAs. We will ask for verification when each campus has met with these groups. How and when you conduct the training is a local campus decision. However, I expect all phases of the training to be completed by February 2.

The School Board adopted a new model of governance during the summer and reaffirmed its commitment on September 15. In the eighteen months we have been working toward full implementation, I have come to appreciate the power and usefulness of this approach to defining what is "Board work" and what is "staff work." Although most groups that work in the area of board governance stress the need to know the difference between setting policy and administering policy, they do not have the comprehensiveness and specificity of this new governance model.

Until now, we have not spent a lot of time on the intricacies of the model. However, I do hope the Board's Results policies are familiar to you.

The Board has set the expectation that our stakeholders—both staff and patrons—have an exposure to this model. To facilitate this awareness effort, we have attached for your use three documents (which will also be provided electronically) that track with three phases of training (which can be accomplished within one and three sessions):

- *Phase One Training*—a Q&A brochure (in English and Spanish) that summarizes the information found on the District web site. (Sufficient copies will be sent to your campus via school mail by the end of next week.)
- *Phase Two Training*—a PowerPoint presentation that goes into more detail about the governance model.
- *Phase Three Training*—a second PowerPoint presentation that outlines the operational policies most relevant to District staff members.

The associate CEOs will be working more closely with you in the very near future to more fully explain the training materials and the specific training objectives and can help answer any questions.

I thank you, in advance, for your help in this matter.

Governance Awareness Initiative
Campus Verification
Your assistance in this matter is most appreciated!

School:
Principal's Signature:

My signature above serves as documentation that my campus has completed the three phases of the governance awareness initiative with the following groups:

1. Campus Staff: (Date)
2. Campus Advisory Council: (Date)
3. PTA: (Date)

Please email or send via school mail this complete and signed form to your associate CEO prior to February 2.

QUESTIONS FOR THOUGHT

1. Which stakeholder groups has your board identified as important to interact with about your new governing system? Which groups deserve priority attention?
2. How will you and/or your CEO communicate to your key administrative staff members the importance of this new governing system and build a relationship that has at its root a common focus on Results?
3. Who in your organizational framework are key opinion leaders who can help build support for your new venture?

FAQS

Q: Should senior staff members be involved with the board as the policies are developed? If we don't do that, how do we get their buy-in after the fact?

A: The choice of who should be in the room when the policies are developed should be made jointly by the board and CEO. We tend to believe it is helpful to the board for key administrative staff to be available throughout, so they understand the GC and BCR policies and as technical advisors as the OE and Results policies are developed. They are to be called upon as needed. If they are involved from the start, less after-the-fact education will be necessary.

Q: If we decide to present our new governance work to citizens, members, and stakeholders, should we start with internal groups before talking to external stakeholders?

A: There really is no right answer, because every organization may have circumstances that make it logical to start with one group over the other. However, as a rule, we recommend starting with key staff and other inside groups, since they can help explain, defend, and advance your work to outside groups with some insider authority.

Q: What do we do if some important people and groups resist our new governing model?

A: Good up-front strategy about the message and how to present it can help minimize that likelihood, but if it happens, the board must be resolute in its commitment to forge ahead. Your ultimate success will be the best means to deflect any opposition. If people or groups oppose what you are doing, assess their reasons. Are those reasons valid, or are they based on misunderstanding? Is their resistance grounded in their fear of losing something? Are there things the board can do to help them overcome their fears or misunderstandings?

And here is a reminder that we have found to be almost unfailingly successful: Focus first and foremost in your discussions on the benefits to those you serve! Improved student achievement; happier seniors living longer and with better health; people with mental or emotional problems feeling safe and understood while their families are also served. It's hard to oppose such universally valued outcomes.

Chapter Three

Monitoring Governance Culture and Board-CEO Relations Policies

The board has identified in its Governance Culture policies its values about how it should do its work. In its Board-CEO Relationship policies, the board has defined how it will function in relationship with its CEO. These two sections of policy actually are operational standards for board behavior. As such, they provide a logical basis for the board to effectively monitor its own performance.

In order for the board to remain faithful to those policies and the performance standards they represent, the board has committed to regularly monitor its performance against those policy standards. Faithful and rigorous self-monitoring of these policies allows the board to:

- Compare its actions with its policy values to determine whether it has performed as it committed to perform;
- Provide a means for self-correction if actions deviate from policy;
- Maintain clarity of roles;
- Model continuing performance improvement; and
- Build capacity for sustainability in the event of board or CEO turnover.

There are a variety of ways to monitor board performance in the Governance Culture and Board-CEO Relations areas. Boards tend to find their own favorite methods, as we have in our coaching relationship with clients. Rather than dwelling on the method, the most important thing is to do it!

Our experience suggests that most boards, regardless of the type of organization they serve, struggle with trying to manage the process without an outside coach or facilitator. Looking at a board's own performance, and judging whether standards were met or not, is difficult to do without an unbiased third party facilitating the discussion.

Our consistent recommendation to boards is that they schedule self-assessments to occur annually at the same time as the CEO's evaluation. Some boards conduct a formative evaluation semiannually to allow for course correction. Still other boards favor a quarterly self-assessment, dividing the policies into four groups for monitoring.

We have found that it is difficult for public boards to effectively self-monitor during a public business meeting, in front of an audience, and often with the cameras rolling. To compound the problem, laws requiring open meetings generally prevent public boards from doing such work in closed sessions.

Options include work sessions, which, although technically "open," usually are not covered by news media or attended by members of the public. Some boards hold premeeting work sessions, which also are technically open, but yet usually enable more free-flowing conversation. Other non-public boards are able to schedule an "executive" or closed session or retreat for the purpose of self-assessment.

Regardless of the environment and timing the board chooses, there are a variety of processes we have found to be successful. Some require members to record their individual conclusions about board compliance in advance, while others require nothing prior to the board's discussion. We discuss below some of the strategies that various boards have used, without any recommendation of a specific one. Readers will find one, or create their own variation, that seems appropriate for them.

EXAMPLE A

Some boards self-monitor by dividing the GC and BCR policies into increments coinciding with the number of meetings the board holds each year, and monitor one or two policies at each meeting. Exhibit 3.1 illustrates how one board collects individual member feedback via a written form prior to each meeting, synthesizes individual responses into one document, and presents it to the whole board at the meeting for discussion and action.

Exhibit 3.1, GC Self-Monitoring Report, is the result of the board's discussion and group action after these individual forms were compiled and discussed. The board uses a Governance Committee, which has recorded the board's action and prepared this summary for the full board. Note that the board has identified why it is noncompliant and what it will do to improve its performance.

To reiterate, we do not recommend that public boards try to self-monitor during a public meeting. If the example cited here is used, discussion and action should be done in some type of session other than a public business meeting.

EXHIBIT 3.1. GC SELF-MONITORING REPORT

GC-7 Annual Board Planning Cycle

To: Board of Trustees
From: Governance Committee
Date:

GC-7 Global Policy Statement:

To accomplish its work with a governance style consistent with board policies, the board will follow an annual agenda that (a) completes a review of Results policies at least biannually, (b) improves its performance through attention to board education and enriched input and deliberation, and (c) completes the monitoring of Operational Expectations policies, Governance Culture policies, and Board-CEO Relationship policies.

GC-7 Policy Subparts:

1. The cycle will conclude each year on the last day of March in order that administrative decisions and budgeting can be based on accomplishing the current board policies.
    In compliance. This year's monitoring cycle begins with our April 8th meeting and will end with the last meeting in March.
2. In the first two months of the new cycle, the board will develop its agenda for the ensuing one-year period.
    In compliance. The board has scheduled on its work plan to adopt the new annual board calendar for the coming year at the first meeting in May.
3. Education, input, and deliberation will receive paramount attention in structuring board meetings and other board activities during the year.
    Not in Compliance. The board has received its first Results monitoring reports in three areas. There has been considerable effort made to allow for the majority of time to be spent evaluating and discussing these reports.
    However, there have been two issues this year that have been in front of the board for an excessive amount of time and have taken away from the board's priority function, which is to address Results for our clients.

Commitment to Improve:

As a result of the excess time spent on these issues, the board will look at its procedure for having items on its agenda for reconsideration. The board did reconstruct its form for Audience Comments in an effort to be more efficient when it receives input from the community.

Approved: Date:

EXAMPLE B

Many boards conduct full self-assessments of all GC and BCR policies at an annual retreat. This self-assessment usually serves as a precursor to the CEO evaluation and the establishment of the board's annual priorities and work plan. To us, it seems logical to conduct the board's self-assessment in conjunction with the CEO evaluation, since the board and CEO are so intimately linked through these policies. It also signifies to the CEO that the board is equally committed to its own improvement.

For both GC and BCR policies, one of the processes we use is a highly visual, no-homework, no-paperwork process. Using such a method allows the board to monitor all GC and BCR policies at one time at an annual retreat. A main benefit of using this process is that it eliminates the paper chase by asking members to talk with each other rather than spending time completing forms.

The process works like this: Prior to the meeting during which the self-assessment occurs, the board's policies are enlarged to fit flip chart–sized paper. We suggest laminating the pages and mounting them on core board for more permanent use. During the meeting, board members are provided a set of colored sticky dots, and each member is asked to place a sticky dot to identify those policies or subsections that the member perceives to be noncompliant. The resulting visual quickly "tees up" those areas that need discussion and action to improve board performance.

The full board discusses the areas that are identified as noncompliant, deciding as a majority whether the board's performance has met expectations and what corrective actions are necessary. A facilitator takes note of the noncompliant policy sections and records any new strategies the board commits to follow to improve its performance. The exercise usually requires about three to four hours to complete, and typically is done in a retreat setting. We recommend that the CEO be included in the process.

Exhibit 3.2 is an illustration of this method. Note that the default choice is "compliant"; dots are placed only where members believe the board has failed to meet the standards it set for itself. These noncompliant provisions of policy become the basis for board discussion and commitment to corrective action.

AN ALTERNATIVE PROCESS

Another process some boards use effectively tends to require even less time. With policy manual in hand, board members are asked to read each GC and BCR policy, then assign a letter grade (A–F) to each policy representing the

EXHIBIT 3.2. GC SELF-MONITORING: VISUAL WITH ENTIRE BOARD

GC-7

Annual Agenda Planning

To accomplish its stated objectives, the Board will follow an annual agenda that schedules continuing review, monitoring and refinement of *Results* policies, engagment meetings with community, student and staff groups, monitoring of policies, and activities to improve Board performance through education, enriched input, and deliberation.

COMPLIANT | NON-COMPLIANT

Accordingly:

1. The planning cycle will end each year in January in order that administrative decision-making and budgeting for the forthcoming year can begin and be based on accomplishing the next one-year segment of the Board's most recent statement of long-term *Results*.

2. The planning cycle will start with the Board's development of its annual agenda for the next year, and will include:

   a. Scheduled dialogue discussions and consultations with selected groups and persons whose insights and opinions will be helpful to the Board;

   b. Discussions on governance matters, including orientation of new Board members in the Board's governance process, and periodic discussions by the Board about means to improve its own performance;

   c. Education related to *Results* policies (e.g., presentations by futurists, demographers, advocacy groups, staff, etc.);

(continued)

> **EXHIBIT 3.2.** *(Continued)*
>
>   d. Scheduled monitoring of all policies.
>
> 3. The Board will take action to update the Agenda Planning Calendar as necessary. A copy of the Calendar is placed in the Board folders at every regularly scheduled meeting.
>
> 4. Throughout the year, the Board will attend to consent agenda items as expeditiously as possible. An item may be removed from the consent agenda only upon approval of a majority of the Board.
>
> 5. Monitoring of *Operational Expectations* policies that were previously accepted by the Board as having been in full compliance will be included on the agenda for separate discussion only if the report indicates Superintendent noncompliance, if a majority of the Board has questions about Superintendent compliance or reasonable interpretation, or if policy content is to be debated. Otherwise *OE* monitoring reports will be included in the consent agenda.

level of performance the member believes the board has demonstrated. After all members have finished their grading exercise, a facilitator asks each member individually to identify for the group the letter assigned to each separate policy, then state why that grade was chosen. Individual member responses are recorded so that all participants can see the grades that have been assigned.

The "why" part of members' answers surfaces the issues and the specific policy subparts the members believe to be noncompliant. This forms the basis for group discussion and resolution of the performance issues. This activity usually requires about three hours and is done in a retreat setting. Again, the facilitator is tasked with developing a document summarizing the board's assessment of its performance and its commitments to corrective actions.

ALTERNATIVES TO SELF-ASSESSMENT: EXTERNAL VERSUS INTERNAL MONITORING

Effectively assessing one's own performance can be difficult, even if the board enjoys the luxury of doing it in a closed session. There are options for boards that have interest in looking at them.

An Outside Consultant

One option is to hire an outside consultant to observe the board in action, examine its processes and documents, interview members and the CEO, and render a third-party assessment based on the findings. This isn't foolproof, however, because sometimes the issues the board itself understands are not readily observable to such third parties who are engaged for short periods of time. Not all performance issues are apparent during board meetings, nor are they necessarily revealed in the documents compiled by the board.

Nevertheless, this is an option that the board might consider in certain circumstances. If the board is primarily concerned, for example, with meeting efficiency or the proper use of parliamentary procedure, it may be appropriate to consider the use of a consultant to assess what is happening and offer recommendations for improvement. This option may not be viable if the board is struggling with interpersonal issues that may not be observable during a brief interaction with the board and its members.

An External Monitoring Committee

One client board we consulted with created a committee of the board to observe each of its meetings and offer appropriate feedback afterward. This "External Monitoring Committee" was comprised of twelve members, representing various elements of the community; it even included some staff members.

We met with the committee after its creation to explain in detail how the board governed and reviewed very carefully the relevant policies that deal with board and board member behavior and expectations. These policies were the standards the committee used to critique the board's performance during meetings. The committee then divided itself into two subcommittees of six persons each. The subcommittees alternated attendance at board meetings.

After each meeting, the subcommittee chair drafted a brief report to the board highlighting the areas of the board's performance the committee felt warranted commendation and those that deserved some attention. Once each quarter, the full committee met with the board for a face-to-face discussion of the highlights and lowlights of the board's work during the previous quarter, as observed by the committee.

This process worked quite well for the board, but there are reasons for that. Members of the committee were appointed because of their integrity and their perceived ability to offer constructive criticism, to be neither full-time critics of—nor cheerleaders for—the board. Committee members were thoroughly trained in and knowledgeable about the board's governing system, and fully prepared to intelligently look for the things that worked and those that did not. And the members were dedicated to the task, which involved substantial amounts of their own time. One report of the committee is shared as a sample in Chapter 9.

IN SUMMARY

These options all are worthy of consideration. As we stated at the beginning of this chapter, there are many ways to self-assess performance against the board's own standards even beyond the options we have discussed here. Boards tend to fare better in self-assessment exercises if they use a third-party facilitator who understands the board's processes and performance standards and who can help manage any personality clashes or interpersonal conflicts that might arise. We emphasize that if a facilitator is used, that person needs to be fully attuned to the governance system the board is using and prepared to offer recommendations appropriate for the system.

What must not be allowed to happen is failure to monitor the board's performance by some process. We have heard these excuses for not doing it: *We have too little time; no one will take it seriously; it's uncomfortable; we might create rifts; we have more important issues to deal with.*

Nevertheless, the board has committed to govern with excellence. Now it must exercise the required maturity and personal discipline to evaluate its performance over time, diagnose problems, and commit to actions for continuous improvement. The board should be just as diligent in assessing its own performance as it is in assessing the performance of the CEO and the organization. Doing so demonstrates the same degree of accountability the board expects from the organization.

QUESTIONS FOR THOUGHT

1. Why is it important for the board to continuously assess its own performance?
2. What is the standard against which the board assesses its performance?
3. What does the board do when its performance fails to meet the standards it has set for itself? What are the repercussions of the board's failure to correct noncompliant conditions?

FAQS

Q: Should senior administrative staff be involved in the board's self-assessment?

A: The presence and participation of staff other than the CEO may not allow for full and open communication between and among members. As a rule, we believe the CEO should participate, but no staff below that level.

Q: What is the best timing for a board self-evaluation?

A: Assuming that all GC and BCR policies are monitored at the same time, it is our experience that the exercise best is done in a board retreat in conjunction with the CEO's summative evaluation.

Q: Should any voting on GC and BCR compliance by individual members be anonymous, or should each member's identity be known?

A: If individuals feel they can't or won't acknowledge their opinions and explain why they voted as they did, it is difficult to have a meaningful conversation that diagnoses problems and activates self-improvement. Therefore, we suggest that all members openly share their opinions with other members of the board.

Chapter Four

Monitoring Operational Expectations Policies

On behalf of the community of owners the board represents and serves, it has worked hard to identify the clear values within which the CEO, and therefore all staff, must make all operational decisions. Operational Expectations policies are the "gold standards for operations" with which the CEO and staff are expected to comply as they make day-to-day decisions for which they have delegated authority.

After the board has defined its standards and delegated operational authority to the CEO, the CEO is required by policy then to monitor operations including these two components:

1. *Reasonably interpret* the board's policy language, including selection of indicators of compliance;
2. *Comply* with the policies' values.

The purpose of Operational Expectations monitoring, stated simply, is to assure the board that the CEO and staff reasonably understand the values underlying the board's policies and to provide data-based evidence that the organization is operating in a compliant manner.

Systematically monitoring OE policies is one of the board's most important functions and one to which it committed in its job description.

The board has delegated substantial authority to the CEO to do his or her job without board interference or approvals. The tradeoff is for the board to receive solid evidence that the CEO's actions and decisions, and those made by every part of the organization, are consistent with the values represented by the policies. This is systemic alignment driven by the board's policies.

This commitment to rigorous monitoring does not mean that every OE monitoring event is a chance to cross-examine or grill the CEO. Some might say that the monitoring process, if abused, is an opportunity for the board to "legally" micromanage the organization.

If the board is using the process to catch the CEO doing something wrong, or if it finds itself so focused on operational monitoring that it compromises its commitment to place Results at the top of the list in importance, the system is being abused.

But the other side of this coin is equally important: Monitoring OE performance should not be a rote action, void of meaning and rigor. Some boards are inclined to *trust* their CEO to do the right thing, and they accept compliance as a default position.

That isn't good enough.

Having trust in the CEO is a good thing, far better than not having trust. *But this system of governance does not depend on trust.* Even if the board has complete confidence and trust in its CEO, it is not doing its job if it fails to require convincing evidence of organizational performance. Some boards appropriately look at the monitoring process as one built on a theme of "trust, but verify."

Spending the time and devoting the effort to build quality monitoring reports can be the point at which a CEO or staff resists. Doing a quality job of monitoring can be time consuming at the start. Some CEOs may ask, "Why doesn't the board just trust me to do my job? Why should we be required to do all this 'extra' work when we have our hands full already?"

This is a two-way system. The board can delegate any degree of authority to the CEO it chooses. But that delegation must be accompanied by solid documentation from its employee, the CEO, that the interpretation of the board's policy is "reasonable" and that compliance has been achieved. Otherwise, the arguments of those who are inclined to criticize the board for excessive delegation are validated.

WHAT CONSTITUTES EFFECTIVE MONITORING?

Monitoring compliance is a formal, planned process, not a random or rote act. Effectively performing this responsibility:

- Assures the board that organizational performance is consistent with the board's values, as expressed in OE policy;
- Allows the board to delegate with assurance that it will know the true operational condition of the organization;

- Provides important information to the board about the operational organization and arms the board with information necessary for its support and advocacy roles;
- Builds one-half of the CEO's annual performance portfolio.

Effective OE monitoring should be viewed as a very positive exercise intended not only to accomplish the objectives listed above, but also to build vital communication between the board and the CEO about the true operational condition of the organization. Since OE monitoring comprises half of the CEO's annual performance evaluation, it should be viewed as a serious obligation to be well executed by both the board and the CEO.

The basic purpose of OE monitoring, again, is to satisfy the board that its policy values are clearly and reasonably understood and are being complied with. Reports should provide ample information for that judgment to be made. If they do not, they should be done again with a reasonable interpretation and information sufficient to allow the board to reach that conclusion.

Although monitoring information must be sufficient for the board to make an informed decision, it need not be exhaustive. Initially, a round or two of reporting by the CEO and responding by the board may be necessary to establish the amount, type, and quality of information required to satisfy the board.

All good OE monitoring reports contain certain required elements in order for the board to make an informed judgment of organizational performance. These elements are:

1. A cover document that includes:
   - An initial statement from the CEO certifying to the board that the report is a true and accurate reflection of the organization's condition;
   - A certification from the CEO to the board of his or her conclusion of the organization's status of compliance, based on the data collected (either in compliance, not in compliance, or in compliance with the exception of identified policy subparts);
   - An executive summary of the report that essentially says, "Here is what you will find in the report"; and
   - A section for the board to record its final action with regard to the report, including any commendations or further actions required of the CEO.

Figure 4.1 is an OE monitoring report cover sheet that captures each of these necessary components. If the purpose of the report is to seek board acceptance of the interpretation and indicators (step one in the monitoring sequence) or if it is to document compliance (step two in the monitoring

(Organization Name)
Operational Expectations Monitoring Document
OE- (#)__ : (Title)

Certification of the CEO: *I certify this report to be accurate*

Signed: _____, CEO   Date: _____

Step One:
__ Approval of Interpretation/Indicators as Reasonable

Step Two: Evidence sufficient to demonstrate
__ Compliance
__ Non-Compliance
__ Compliance with Noted Exceptions Below

_____
_____
_____

Executive Summary:

Disposition of the Board:

__ Approval of Interpretation/Indicators as Reasonable
__ In Compliance
__ Not in Compliance
__ Compliance with Noted Exceptions

Summary statement/motion of the Board:
_____
_____

Signed: _____, President   Date: _____ Re-monitor: _____

Figure 4.1. Operational Expectations Monitoring Document

sequence), the appropriate purpose can be readily identified by the CEO in the lines following the CEO's signature.

2. Section-by-section information:
   The full policy-monitoring document (see Appendices A & B for samples) will include a restatement of the board's policy, section by section. Each restated section is followed by:
   - The CEO's literal interpretation of the board's policy provision, and in addition, identified quantifiable "indicators" the CEO will use to judge compliance;
   - An indication of organizational condition with regard to that specific policy provision—either in compliance or out of compliance;
   - Evidence of that condition, using data based on the indicators; and
   - If out of compliance, an explanation of the reasons for that condition, information about what is being done to gain compliance, and the projected date for compliance to be achieved.

WHY ALL THE FUSS ABOUT INTERPRETATION AND INDICATORS?

Interpretation of the board's policy language, and the related identification of indicators, is the critical pivot point of a good monitoring report. This is why: People don't respond to the words we use; they respond to *their interpretation* of the words we use. The board must be assured that the language it has used in stating its policies is being reasonably interpreted. That interpretation drives not only the organization's actions, but also the CEO's choice of indicators and the body of compliance data.

An example: In several places in most board policy manuals, the value of "safety" is stated. The board wants working conditions to be safe, the learning environment to be safe, and all buildings to be safe. What does that term, *safe*, mean? Does it mean that no individual ever will be harmed or injured at any time under any circumstances? If so, no organization ever could be compliant.

If that interpretation is unreasonable, what are the alternatives? What is a reasonable interpretation of that value that allows the organization to achieve compliance? How "safe" does a workplace need to be before it is compliant? Or how "unsafe" must it be before it is noncompliant?

Ultimately, the CEO is obligated to report to the board that the organization either is compliant or noncompliant with the stated value of "safe." How will that judgment be made?

This all depends upon how "safe" is interpreted, and the indicators that have been selected to measure whether actual conditions are safe. It all revolves around the interpretation of the board's value, and whether or not the board and CEO are in agreement with the reasonable standard of interpretation.

LITERAL INTERPRETATION OF THE BOARD'S LANGUAGE

Let's look at each part of this interpretation component separately, beginning with the literal interpretation. In developing an interpretation, the CEO *never* should use the same words the board used in its policy. Simply restating the same words fails to tell the board whether the CEO understands the underlying value of the policy. The board deserves to know what "safe" means to the CEO as the staff applies that value to operational conditions.

The CEO might respond in a monitoring report by applying the following interpretation to the term: "I interpret 'safe' to mean '*organizational conditions that protect against physical, emotional, or psychological danger or harm and that provide reasonable assurance that employees and others are unlikely to sustain such harm*.'" This interpretation could be extended to specify the physical and operational areas included in the application of the word, such as "*at all buildings and sites and all off-site activities for which the organization is responsible*," for example.

This interpretation does not guarantee that no one ever will be injured at a site or during an activity under the control of the organization. But if data collected indicate that people are being injured on property controlled by the organization, one might conclude that conditions failed to adequately protect against such risks and therefore the organization is noncompliant.

If that is the case, just how many people can be injured before the organization becomes noncompliant? And what kinds of injury, under what circumstances, should be factored into the equation? Remember, perfection is not the standard; the standard is *reasonable*.

What should be interpreted? Each separate subpart of every OE policy is its own "smaller policy," and therefore each subpart requires its own interpretation (see Appendices A & B examples). But within each policy subpart, the CEO is obligated to interpret every key word and phrase. We used the example of "safe" earlier. That is a key word, which requires careful interpretation.

So might the phrase "provide adequate information to ensure informed board decisions," typically found in the board's OE policy on Communication with the Board. This series of words constitutes a specific value stated by the board. What is the value underlying those words? Why would a board feel the need to say this? The interpretation should be sufficient to assure the board that the CEO understands why the board values that kind and degree of information. We encourage the CEO to use the following introductory fragment to guide the interpretation: *"The board values . . .,"* followed by the CEO's understanding of the board's underlying value.

INTERPRETATIONS DRIVE SELECTION OF INDICATORS

The second part of the interpretation, indicators, is at least as important as the literal interpretation. Referring back to an OE policy addressing safety, which indicators will the CEO and staff use to judge whether the organization is in compliance with the board's value of safety? What is a reasonable performance standard?

We encourage the CEO to use the following introductory fragment to make that determination: *"We will know we are compliant when . . ."* In other words, what tangible, observable, and documentable conditions must exist in order for compliance to be demonstrated?

The sentence may be completed by such options as the following:

- *"the number of workers' compensation claims filed by employees during the year is five or fewer."* Or,
- *"the number of students sustaining serious injury on school property during the year is two or fewer at any school site."* Or,
- *"fire department inspections reveal zero major violations and two or fewer minor exceptions to the fire code at all sites during the year."*

The important thing to note about these indicators is that all are very precise and quantifiable. Selecting quantifiable indicators has the distinct advantage of eliminating any later argument about whether the organization is compliant. If data collected against the indicator hit the identified standard, then by definition compliance has been achieved.

It is conceivable that the board may agree that compliance has been achieved even if the target number was missed slightly. But when the indicator is tied with a number as this example suggests, it has the effect of predetermining what compliance is and should make the actual monitoring decision much less subjective.

If the board has accepted the choice of indicators as a part of the CEO's interpretation, and if internal monitoring processes reveal that the performance targets were realized, then the organization is, by definition, compliant.

If the numbers were not realized, based on data collected from multiple indicators, the board likely would consider the organization to be noncompliant, and improvement is expected. Unless there are some justifiable aberrations to be considered, there should be little or no debate about the condition of the organization, either by the board or by the staff.

The board always has the final decision about whether such an interpretation is reasonable. But it is important to remember the standard for interpretation the board stated in its policy: It is *reasonable*. The board did not say that it would accept only interpretations that it considers "perfect," or those that meet the personal preferences of individual members. There are many ways to interpret "safe," and the number of potential indicators is large.

The *reasonable* standard must be applied each time the judgment is made, or the board is back in the micromanagement business. If the CEO presents to the board an interpretation or proposed indicators that the board or some of its members consider unreasonable, the temptation will be to substitute the board's choices for those of the CEO.

Avoid that at all costs.

Amending a CEO report to substitute the board's preferences means that the board is doing the CEO's work, and therefore accountability is transferred back to the board. Remember the principle: *"S/he who makes a decision is accountable for the result."*

A board with which we once were familiar became so frustrated with the poor monitoring reports it was receiving from its CEO that it chose to form a committee of board members to write the interpretations of the board's Operational Expectations policies. Individual members had strong opinions about what they should be, and the CEO had been unable to meet those board members' expectations. In taking this action, however, the board essentially assumed responsibility for reporting on operational performance in the areas covered by the reports, leaving the CEO free from accountability.

If a report is considered unreasonable by a majority of the board, the board should not accept it, and should return it to the CEO with the expectation that the CEO and staff resubmit a report that is reasonable. One would hope that such a process is rarely required. But returning a report is far better than the board's substituting its decisions for those that belong to the CEO.

Figure 4.2 is a partial OE monitoring report that includes both interpretations and indicators. This example does not yet include actual monitoring data. It reflects the first step in a two-step monitoring sequence, which we discuss in more detail below. The format of this report is one we recommend; it is simple, clear, and concise.

Operational Expectations Monitoring Document
OE-8: Asset Protection
Reasonable Interpretation and Indicators

Certification of the Superintendent: I certify this report to be accurate

Signed: _____, Superintendent   Date: _____

_____ Request Approval of Interpretation/Indicators as Reasonable

Disposition of the Board: Date: _____ Re-monitoring: _____

_____ Approval of Interpretations/Indicators as Reasonable
_____ In Compliance
_____ Not in Compliance
_____ Compliance with Noted Exceptions

Summary statement/motion of the Board:
_____
_____
_____

President: _____, Superintendent: _____

Figure 4.2. Operational Expectations Monitoring Document

OE-8: Asset Protection	Superintendent		BoE	
	In Compliance	Not in Compliance	In Compliance	Not in Compliance
The Superintendent will assure that all district assets are adequately protected, properly maintained, appropriately used and not placed at undue risk.				
Superintendent Interpretation: • *District assets* shall mean all property and equipment that is tangible in nature with a life longer than one year owned by the District that cost more than $5,000. • *Adequately protected* shall mean insured for 100% replacement value. • *Properly maintained* shall mean serviced and repaired on a regular basis to retain in good operating condition. • *Appropriately used* shall mean as trained by district personnel in compliance with operating guidelines established by the manufacturer. • *Not placed at undue risk* shall mean safe from actions that would cause District assets to be harmed or damaged or create an unsafe environment.				
Board Comments:				
OE-8.1 The Superintendent will maintain property and casualty insurance coverage on district property with limits equal to 100% of replacement value.				
SUPERINTENDENT Interpretation: • *Property* shall mean facilities, vehicles, equipment, and materials with an insurable risk. • *100% of replacement value* shall mean the ability to replace and make whole property losses experienced by the District subject to any and all deductibles.				

Figure 4.2. *Continued*

SUPERINTENDENT Indicators of Compliance: We will know we are compliant when: • The District purchases and receives the coverage declarations for property and casualty insurance equal to 100% of replacement value. SUPERINTENDENT Evidence of Compliance:			
Board Comments:			
OE-8.2 The Superintendent will maintain both Errors and Omissions and Comprehensive General Liability insurance coverage protecting board members, staff and the district itself in an amount that is reasonable for school districts of comparable size and character. Section 24-10-101, C.R.S.			
SUPERINTENDENT Interpretation: • *Errors and Omissions insurance* shall mean protection for board members and staff who make a mistake in performing their duties in good faith and results in harm to the District. • *Comprehensive General Liability insurance* shall mean protection against bodily injury and property damage claims. • *Amount that is reasonable* shall mean the value of the insurance pool. • *Comparable size and character* shall mean other school districts with similar numbers of students and at-risk factors.			
SUPERINTENDENT Indicators of Compliance: We will know we are compliant when: • The District has purchased and receives the coverage declarations for Errors and Omissions and Comprehensive General Liability insurance coverage. SUPERINTENDENT Evidence of Compliance:			
Board Comments:			

Figure 4.2. *Continued*

OE-8.3 The Superintendent will assure that all personnel who have access to material amounts of district and school funds are covered under the district general liability and crime policy.			
SUPERINTENDENT Interpretation: • *All personnel* shall mean any district employee. • *Material amounts* shall mean more than $500, which is equivalent to the deductible amount. • *General liability and crime policy* shall mean District rules and regulations regarding loss or damage to money, securities and other property resulting directly from theft committed by an employee whether identified or not, acting alone or in collusion with other persons.			
SUPERINTENDENT Indicators of Compliance: We will know we are compliant when: • The District has purchased and receives the coverage declarations for crime coverage and the policy has been received. SUPERINTENDENT Evidence of Compliance:			
Board Comments:			
OE-8.4 The Superintendent will protect intellectual property, information, files, records and fixed assets from loss or significant damage.			
SUPERINTENDENT Interpretation: • *Intellectual property* shall mean creations of the mind: inventions, literary and artistic works, and symbols, names, images, and designs used in commerce. • *District intellectual property* shall mean original curriculum, teaching materials, or other documents created by district employees as part of			

Figure 4.2. *Continued*

their job for use by the District or its employees.

- *Information, files and records* shall mean electronic data on District servers deemed critical (Finance, Human Capital, Student Support and Research, Data & Accountability) to the operations of the District.

- *Fixed assets* shall mean property and equipment with original cost of $5,000 or more.

- With regard to fixed assets, *significant damage* shall mean harm or destruction requiring more than $5,000 of unplanned repair or maintenance including labor, material, and equipment rental costs.

SUPERINTENDENT Indicators of Compliance:
We will know we are compliant when:

- The District receives no legal complaints that its employees have violated intellectual property rights.

- Information, files, and records are backed up each night and there is no loss of these files and records during the school year.

- The District repairs or replaces all fixed assets impaired by significant damage during the school year.

- The District has offsite storage (servers housed in a different District facility or vendor facility) or onsite fireproof safe storage of all technology data and a recovery plan for loss of information, files and records.

- District intellectual property used by other school districts is used with the permission of either the Curriculum, Instruction and Assessment Department or the Superintendent.

SUPERINTENDENT Evidence of Compliance:

Figure 4.2. *Continued*

Board Comments:				
OE-8.5 The Superintendent may not allow facilities and equipment to be subject to improper use or insufficient maintenance.				
SUPERINTENDENT Interpretation: • *Facilities and equipment* shall mean assets in excess of $5,000 original cost. • *Improper use* shall mean inappropriate operation or treatment, or utilization in a manner or for a purpose contrary to what was intended. • *Insufficient maintenance* shall mean inadequate repair, cleaning, inspection, or upkeep as recommended by manufactured specifications.				

Figure 4.2. *Continued*

SUPERINTENDENT Indicators of Compliance:
We will know we are compliant when:

- No person is injured in one of the District's facilities or when using District equipment as a result of insufficient maintenance of the facility or equipment.

- Workmen's compensation claims filed as a result of the improper use of equipment does not exceed ten claims in the school year.

- The District maintains and adheres to a long-range capital preventative maintenance plan to help guide the prioritization of Capital Reserve Fund appropriations.

SUPERINTENDENT Evidence of Compliance:

Board Comments:

OE-8.6 The Superintendent may not recklessly expose the district, the Board or staff to legal liability.

SUPERINTENDENT Interpretation:

- *Recklessly expose* shall mean to commit an offence that is grossly negligent putting the District in a legally untenable position which cost

Figure 4.2. *Continued*

the District more than $10,000.

- *Legal liability* shall mean legal judgments against the district resulting from actions taken by the superintendent.

SUPERINTENDENT Indicators of Compliance:
We will know we are compliant when:

- The District incurs no legal costs or damage awards as a result of careless and reckless acts by the Superintendent.

SUPERINTENDENT Evidence of Compliance:

Board Comments:

OE-8.7 The Superintendent may not invest funds in investments that are not secured or that are not authorized by law.

SUPERINTENDENT Interpretation:

- *Funds* shall mean money or capital.

- *Investments* shall mean the commitment of District money or capital to the purchase of financial instruments or other assets so as to gain profitable returns in the form of interest, income, dividend, or appreciation of the value of the instrument.

SUPERINTENDENT Indicators of Compliance:
We will know we are compliant when:

- All investments are in compliance with State Statute and the auditor's management letter makes no comment in regards to investments.

- The District has only deposited funds with entities govened by Public Depository Protection Act and District investment policy.

SUPERINTENDENT Evidence of Compliance:

Figure 4.2. *Continued*

Board Comments:				
OE-8.8 The Superintendent may not purchase or sell real estate, including land and buildings.				
SUPERINTENDENT Interpretation: • *Purchase* shall mean to obtain ownership of an asset in exchange for money or value. • *Sell* shall mean to surrender ownership of an asset in exchange for money or value.				
SUPERINTENDENT Indicators of Compliance: We will know we are compliant when: • All dispositions and acquisitions of land and buildings are approved by board resolution. • There will be no audit finding by the independent external auditors in reference to improper disposition and acquisition of land and buildings. SUPERINTENDENT Evidence of Compliance:				
Board Comments:				

Indicators

Figure 4.2. *Continued*

OE MONITORING PROCESS

When the board is first launching its practice of Coherent Governance, we recommend a two-step process for monitoring OE policies. This is why: If the CEO's interpretation, including the choice of indicators, is not considered reasonable by the board, monitoring data tied to that unreasonable interpretation and indicators very likely will be unacceptable to the board. If the interpretation and indicators are unreasonable, those problems will not be solved by adding monitoring data to the equation.

As a first step, we believe it is preferable to have the board and CEO establish common understanding about the reasonable interpretation and compliance indicators that will be used. It is at the second step, which comes later, that the CEO presents actual monitoring data aligned with the interpretation and chosen indicators.

Step One

In the first step of this two-step monitoring process, the CEO presents only a reasonable interpretation of the policy and each of its subparts, along with compliance indicators. These indicators are intended to measure the observable, and preferably quantifiable, conditions that the CEO plans to use to judge whether the organization is compliant.

The board should judge the interpretation and indicators *based on whether the board considers them to be reasonable*. This action assures the CEO that when compliance information is presented later, that information will be based upon an interpretation and indicators that already have been accepted by the board. Again, we caution against the board's taking any action other than either:

1. to accept the interpretation and indicators as reasonable, or
2. to return them to the CEO for another attempt if the board finds them to be unreasonable.

Step Two

In the second step, the CEO finalizes the report by presenting compliance data against the board's previously accepted interpretation and indicators. Since the data are based on the indicators and the selected performance targets, this final piece should be the simplest and least debatable part of the process.

There should be a reasonable time interval between the first and second steps in order for the CEO to effectively assess the organization's actual condition and to compile documentation for the compliance report.

Although this two-step sequence may slow the implementation process a bit during the first year, the delay should not be a major factor in the long run. This sequence applies only to the first monitoring cycle. The second and subsequent monitoring cycles can omit the first step of presenting the interpretation and indicators for separate board acceptance, since it is likely the interpretations and indicators previously accepted by the board remain reasonable. Any performance targets that are included as a part of the quantifiable indicators could be adjusted after each monitoring event based on actual performance.

On a continuing basis, monitoring reports should continue to include all components previously accepted by the board (interpretation and indicators), but the primary focus now is on the monitoring data as evidence of compliance.

DISPOSITION OF THE BOARD

Once the monitoring report is presented, the board should formally act on it through a vote. Board action should result in one of the following choices:

1. Compliance
2. Not in compliance
3. Compliance with noted exception(s)

The board's vote is recorded on the monitoring report cover, along with any amending motions (such as action to commend or scheduled remonitoring of the whole or a subpart), in order to serve as a record.

These monitoring report covers, reflecting the board's action, will be of major importance at the end of the monitoring cycle when overall judgments are made about the organization's—and the CEO's—performance during the preceding year. At that point, the board should not try to review the complete reports it has judged during the year, but rather it should be able to review the report covers only as a means to refresh its thinking about how each operational report was received and decided by the board and to develop summative judgments of organizational and CEO performance.

This action closes the loop on that particular monitoring event. The monitoring document and board summary cover become a part of the CEO's cumulative performance portfolio.

In Appendices A & B, we have included completed monitoring reports that can serve as a model for your own work.

ADVICE FOR THE CEO ABOUT OE MONITORING

Building a quality monitoring report requires the CEO and supporting executive staff members to take the responsibility seriously. It is an important exercise, not only because it serves as the basis for the board's judgment of the organization's performance, but also because it provides the opportunity for the CEO and staff to examine the real condition of every operational function at least once each year.

When reports are developed, we suggest that the CEO:

- *Use a consistent format*, following the content steps we outlined at the top of this section and reflected in the examples (see Figure 4.2). Present the steps in their *natural order* as shown. Board members must be able to understand quickly and easily what the reports contain without having to sift through multiple presentation formats and styles.
- *Treat each subpart of the policy as a separate policy.* Each deserves its own interpretation, indicators, and evidence of compliance.
- *Be absolutely, brutally honest in assessing compliance.* If the organization is not in compliance, say so. The board must be able to rely on the CEO's word. It takes only one instance of falsifying a report to destroy the board's confidence in both the process and the CEO. *It usually is not a capital offense to be out of compliance; however, it is a capital offense to intentionally mislead or falsify information!*
- *Adhere to timelines.* If the board's annual work plan calls for a report to be provided by a given date, don't let that date pass without submitting it. If delays must occur for good reason, the board should agree with any resulting change to its own calendar.
- *Avoid presenting process disguised as evidence.* This is the number-one problem we see with OE monitoring reports. The CEO and staff understandably are eager to let the board know all the wonderful things the organization is doing. But processes do not matter here. *What the board must receive is solid evidence that all those great things the staff has done actually worked.* The monitoring report should let the board know that they did. That means that compliance must be demonstrated by actual performance data, not by process information and a list of staff efforts and activities.
- *Include process (optional).* If reports do include process information, it should be clearly labeled as *incidental information* or *for board information only*, and it should be placed at the end of the report as an appendix. Do not mix compliance data with process information. If this option to document and share process is chosen, it should be for the purpose of educating the board.

The OE monitoring report can be a very effective vehicle to share information about processes and practices that otherwise the board would never know. But it should always be recognized that *process does not equal evidence*. Do not confuse activity with compliance Results.
- *Sharing capacity building (optional)*. Listing capacities that the organization needs to develop in order to improve its performance can be useful, especially if the organization is noncompliant in a given area due to limited resources. It can be helpful to share with the board the conditions that must change in order for compliance to be achieved. Such information should identify the needed resources, and the projected time frame necessary, for the organization to achieve and document full compliance or to further improve operational performance and accountability.

The Palm Springs Unified School District Human Resources Department found itself unable to adequately document compliance with the board's OE policy on Personnel Administration due to outdated technology. In a capacity-building section of the organization's monitoring report, the CEO identified the need for new technology systems and adequate employee training. The board agreed with the need to build that increased internal capacity, and the noncompliance status was not "faulted" to the CEO during the period of time that was required to improve that organizational capability.

DISPOSE OF REPORTS ON THE CONSENT AGENDA OR AS SEPARATE ACTION ITEMS?

Some boards have asked the question about whether to dispose of OE monitoring reports via consent agenda if there are no concerns about the report, since the board has made the commitment in policy to spend most of its time focused on Results. It is a fair question, especially if the board has adopted a customary practice of not talking about matters it believes do not warrant discussion time.

But this effort to save time is ill advised for an activity as important as judging whether the organization is meeting the board's operational standards.

We already have underscored the significant importance of OE monitoring. It should not be taken lightly. This does not mean that the board should spend an hour of every meeting discussing an OE monitoring report, especially when the board has committed in policy to focus its primary attention on Results performance.

Each OE report submitted to the board represents many hours of CEO and staff time gathering information to document compliance. In return, the board owes the CEO a thoughtful and fair response based on a thorough review of the data and consideration of conclusions reached on the basis of that data. This means that some board meeting time is necessary in order to provide that quality response.

The first year especially is important, since this is the learning period. It is crucial for both the board and CEO to take the time to review and discuss each report openly to gain familiarity with the policy content and to establish an acceptable level of communication between the parties.

TWO CRITICAL REALITIES TO CONSIDER IN HAVING AN OPEN DISCUSSION ON OE REPORTS

First: Turnover Happens

Orienting new members and key staff to the critical policy content and accountability inherent to the monitoring process is crucial to the sustainability of the CG system. New people coming into an organization may think they understand the board's governance processes, but they may not fully appreciate the significance of the reports.

We have experienced new CEOs who have come close to asking the board to "trust me" by burying inadequate reports or reports that reflect negatively on operational performance in consent agendas in order to diminish quality board attention to them. Such actions lead to the slippery slope of sloppy accountability, and the extinction cycle begins.

New board members also can undermine systemic accountability. They may not understand or embrace the significance of effective monitoring. They may be familiar only with traditional governance methods and see little value in spending time on "more reports." This underscores the extreme importance of quality orientation of new members to help them understand why the board systematically monitors operations rather than injecting itself into operational decision-making when problems occur and become the crisis du jour.

Second: Public Understanding Is Needed

For public boards, public understanding of the board's accountability system must be taken into consideration. If OE reports are not publicly and openly presented and judged, the board risks being accused of giving away its power. Staff, public, and the media all should hear, see, and feel the board systematically judging organizational compliance with its high standards for operations.

GETTING TO RESULTS

We caution boards against dwelling too long and too intently on this "new toy." Some boards can consume themselves with OE monitoring, and as a result find themselves back in a place they said they wanted to leave: mired in the intimate details of organizational operations.

As a rule of thumb, OE monitoring should take less board meeting time than the board's attention to Results. If OE monitoring seems to be the centerpiece of the board's meeting, the board probably is too focused on OE monitoring—unless operationally something seriously is not working.

CEO or Organization Evaluation?

What the board is doing when it acts on an OE monitoring report is expressing its satisfaction—or lack thereof—with the *organization's* performance. The starting point for OE monitoring is a review of the organization's performance, *not* the CEO's performance. The CEO's personal evaluation will occur in a separate, and usually closed, session when the summative evaluation is conducted at the end of the monitoring cycle. This issue is discussed more fully in Chapter 6.

PRESENTING THE MONITORING REPORT

There is something of an art to effectively presenting and acting on a monitoring report, both for Operational Expectations and Results policies. Most boards have not previously engaged in a process quite like this, so it can feel awkward at first.

This awkward phase should pass very quickly, however, once the board gains comfort as a result of doing it a time or two. The best way we have found to effectively dispose of monitoring reports is to follow established parliamentary procedure, according to the processes recommended below.

The process example that follows assumes that the report being presented is a formal monitoring report, including acceptance of both interpretation and compliance data, as outlined at the beginning of this chapter.

The board president begins the board's consideration by contextualizing the report, introducing it with comments similar to the following:

> "The board has established through its Operational Expectations policies its values about how this organization is expected to operate. We have clearly expressed the conditions that must exist as business is conducted.
>
> "We now will receive the CEO's monitoring report on our Operational Expectation policy (OE-5, Financial Planning and Budget). We will receive the

report containing the CEO's interpretation of our language, a certification of current conditions, and monitoring data. This monitoring action constitutes our rigorous oversight of the organization and assures the board that its operational standards have been met. I now recognize (CEO) for the purpose of presenting a summary of the report."

The CEO "tees up" the report by stating the operational area being monitored, and he or she reminds the board of the action being requested of it. The CEO presents a brief summary of the report, or s/he may introduce a staff member who had the "point position" for preparing it. *The CEO or designee should not read the report to the board*, but rather summarize it by highlighting its important points and conclusions—a verbal executive summary—much as is reported on the cover sheet of the report. Board members should not interrupt the CEO's presentation, but save their questions and comments until the overview is complete.

AFTER THE REPORT HAS BEEN PRESENTED

Following the overview of the report, the president should ask members if there are any questions for the CEO or the staff member who prepared the report. The objective is for the board to gain a full understanding of the report and to satisfy itself that the CEO has addressed all significant issues.

At this point, the report still belongs to the CEO, not to the board. The board needs to assure itself that it has sufficient information and understanding necessary to fairly dispose of the report at the next level.

Following the Q&A with the CEO, the president should close this section of the discussion by reminding the board of its policy standard for accepting these reports (BCR-5) with a statement similar to the following:

> "Members of the board have received and discussed the CEO's monitoring report on OE-___. Now it is the board's responsibility to consider the report as evidence of organization performance in this area of operations. Let me remind the board of the criteria we should use to judge this report. They are whether the board is satisfied that:
>
> 1. The CEO's interpretation of the policy is reasonable;
> 2. The CEO has provided sufficient evidence to assure the board that the organization is in compliance with the provisions of the policy;
> 3. Or if noncompliance is being reported, whether the CEO has disclosed procedures and a timeline to establish compliance.
>
> "I will now entertain a motion to accept and approve the report as presented by the CEO."

In order to start board discussion of a monitoring report, we recommend a motion similar to the following:

> *"Mr./Madam President, I move to accept and approve the CEO's monitoring report on OE-_ as presented by the CEO."*

This "clean" motion is appropriate, even if there are interpretation or compliance issues to be considered. The routine amendment process may be used to express any such concerns.

Once a member moves to accept and approve the report, ownership of the report now has shifted from the CEO to the board. In other words, discussion of the report now is among members of the board, not between the board and CEO. If there are no amending motions or issues to be discussed, the board simply votes, after which the report has been accepted as presented.

If a member believes that a specific part of the report is unreasonable or that compliance has not been demonstrated, the member initiates an amending motion to exclude that section of the report from the motion to approve. The motion might be similar to the following:

Possible Amending Motion

> *"Mr./Madam President, I move to amend the motion by excluding (insert specific part of report the mover believes to be unreasonable or noncompliant)."*

✓ Second, then discuss and vote on the amendment.
✓ Specific details should be offered by the mover to justify the change.
✓ A date for possible remonitoring of the exception should be scheduled.

Follow parliamentary procedure. Faithfully start the discussion with a motion and second, as suggested above, in order to frame the discussion and possible amending motions leading to final board action.

After board discussion and action, the final vote is recorded on the cover of the OE report. That action should be one of three possible options:

a. *In compliance*
b. *In compliance with noted exceptions.* This means that any policy subparts reported as noncompliant, or any subparts excluded by the board from the motion to approve, are scheduled for remonitoring at a defined time.
c. *Not in compliance*, with a defined follow-up date for remonitoring the entire policy.

If a remonitoring date is determined, it is added to the report cover and to the board's annual work plan immediately. This assures the board that the necessary follow-up action will take place. The administrative assistant to the board, or the board clerk, will find that the annual work plan could change at every meeting of the board.

This is the time for the board to express commendation, concern, or criticism and to provide any official feedback it believes appropriate relative to this area of operational performance. These points should be summarized and recorded by the administrative assistant in the minutes and added to the report's cover sheet under the president's signature. Remember that the board's findings and vote on the cover sheet will be critical for compiling the later summative CEO evaluation.

If your board is a public board, such as a school board, we recommend having a written executive summary of the report available for audience members to use to follow the board's discussion. The board also might consider projecting the relevant policy title and opening preamble on large, readable screens. Some boards have copies of all of their policies, duplicated in small binders, available at board meetings for public use.

The sample monitoring reports contained in the Appendices are intended to help your board start its journey toward a meaningful experience in this important segment of implementation.

SOME POINTS TO CONSIDER

- *Remember, again, that the standard of organization performance the board has set in policy is reasonable, not perfection.* Both the board and CEO are doing something they never have done before, and some less-than-perfect work is to be expected in the early going.

    In some cases, the organization may be performing in a very compliant manner, but lack the organizational capacity at this early stage to prove it. Thus the message to both the board and CEO is to be tolerant of each other as this process is being institutionalized.

    This is not to suggest that clearly substandard performance be accepted. This is a serious process, and it deserves the CEO's best effort to produce a quality monitoring report, fairly documenting the true condition of the organization's operational performance.

    Assuming the CEO has given a good-faith effort, the board might recognize that effort, and state its expectation that the reports will improve and that documentation will become stronger when presented the second and third time.

- *We remind the CEO that neither the report nor any accompanying PowerPoint presentations should be read verbatim to the board.* Assume that each

member has done the required homework. Provide an executive summary of the important points contained in the report.
- To both board and CEO, remember that *this monitoring process is not intended to be a negative event, nor an opportunity to catch someone doing something wrong.* It is intended to be an opportunity to critically but constructively examine what is working as expected and where new attention might be needed. It is truth-telling between the board and the CEO as a means to improvement.
- If the report acknowledges noncompliance with any part of the policy, the *CEO also should inform the board of specific plans to remedy the noncompliant condition and the timeline necessary to achieve compliance.* Board acceptance of the report includes its acknowledgment of the noncompliant conditions and its agreement with the timeline for remedy.
- *Avoid using the reports as opportunities to second-guess the CEO or to do the CEO's work for him or her.* We again caution the board against spending an inordinate amount of time disposing of OE reports. Take as much time as reasonably necessary to be sure you understand what the report says and whether you are convinced that organizational performance is reasonably compliant.
- *Remember: The board's job is not to substitute its opinions for those of the CEO.* The task is to either accept the report as presented, accept the parts considered compliant and exclude (by amendment) the parts considered to be noncompliant, or return the entire report to the CEO for additional work. If the board substitutes its own opinions and ideas for those of the CEO, it is doing the CEO's work. That is something that never should happen. This system of governance hinges on absolute role clarity.
- *If the board considers parts of the report to be noncompliant, they are excluded by amendment from the compliance motion and a date for remonitoring of those parts of the policy should be established.* Dialogue between the board and CEO ensures a reasonable timeline for remonitoring of the report. The remonitoring event is placed on the board's annual work plan to ensure that it does not fall between the cracks. If it is a critical noncompliant condition, the board may choose to remonitor in short order. If the noncompliant condition is relatively minor, the board may choose to delay remonitoring until the next regularly scheduled cycle.
- *The board can choose to directly monitor an operational area, or alternatively, to engage an outside expert for external monitoring.* As outlined in our first book, *Good Governance Is a Choice,* the means by which an operational area is monitored is always the choice of the board, even though the default method is the internal report. The board already relies on external monitoring to an extent when a financial audit is conducted

on Financial Administration. Monitoring other operational functions by external review can be performed at any time if the board feels the need for someone outside of the organization with expertise to examine performance and determine the state of compliance.

ORGANIZING STAFF

Well before the first report is prepared by the CEO and presented to the board, the CEO must organize the staff to support the process. How to do that is dependent largely on the size of the staff and the complexity of the organization. Exhibit 4.1, a staff alignment chart, was developed by one CEO to schedule the staff's work as they prepared reports for ultimate presentation to the board.

Exhibit 4.1. Sample OE Report Prep Schedule

OE Policy	Staff Responsible	Date for Review by Cabinet	Date Due to Board	Date to Be on Board Agenda
2: Emergency CEO Succession	CEO	July 14	July 25	August 11
5: Financial Planning	CFO	August 11	August 22	September 8
6: Financial Administration	CFO	August 25	September 5	September 22
1: Global Operational Expectation	CEO	September 15	September 26	October 13
8: Communication with the Board	Director of Comm	September 31	October 10	October 27
4: Personnel Administration	Director of HR	October 10	October 24	November 10
3: Treatment of Stakeholders	Director of HR	October 24	November 7	November 10
9: Communicating with the Public	Director of Comm	October 24	November 7	November 24
10: Instructional Program	Director of Instruction	November 7	November 21	December 8
12: Facilities	Director of Facilities	November 29	December 12	January 12
7: Asset Protection	CFO	December 15	January 9	January 26
11: Learning Environment	Director of Instruction	January 12	January 23	February 9

Notes:
- senior staff assigned by CEO
- review at Monday cabinet meetings, with two weeks to revise and submit to consultants
- consultant review return to point person
- reports due to board on Fridays, approximately two weeks prior to board meeting

In some organizations of modest size, this degree of staff delegation may not be necessary or possible. But in larger organizations, it is desirable to create as many opportunities as possible for first- and second-tier executive staff members to engage in the process. This involvement builds capacity and ownership by involving good minds in support of the entire organizational response to the board's policies.

Planning this process should begin with the end in mind. By what date should the report be delivered to the board in sufficient time for members to read, study, and analyze the content? How much time should be planned for board members to ask any questions for clarification prior to the meeting at which the report will be presented and deliberated? Board members commonly expect a week to ten days to study monitoring reports.

As staff work schedules are developed, the CEO should consider designating a point person to be responsible for each report, based on logical staff responsibilities and organizational alignment. The draft report should be submitted to the administrative cabinet or senior leadership team for critique and group feedback in time to permit revisions before it is submitted to the board. After cabinet review, some boards send the resulting report to consultants for "third-eye" feedback before it is finalized and submitted to the board.

This is a time when the board's administrative assistant or other designated support person is invaluable for ensuring that all staff reports are prepared on time to deliver according to the board's annual work plan. Someone must be designated to quarterback this entire process, to drive it according to schedule. If that person isn't the CEO, he or she must have sufficient authority to require other staff members to deliver the necessary documents at the required time. Otherwise, the best of schedules on paper becomes meaningless exercises.

QUESTIONS FOR THOUGHT

1. Why should a board be diligent in monitoring operational performance? Does doing so demonstrate lack of trust in the CEO?
2. How do boards operating in a traditional governing environment exercise confident control over all operations of the organization?
3. Should a CEO develop monitoring reports in isolation from senior staff? Why would that not be advisable?

FAQS

Q: Isn't requiring the CEO and staff to struggle with an interpretation a waste of staff time when the words in the policy seem quite clear on their face?

A: No. Words mean something—and sometimes something different from one person to another. The interpretation is important, because it assures the board that communication of the same value has occurred and that organizational response to the board's policy will be acceptable to the board. The time to determine whether interpretations are reasonable is before any missteps occur, not afterward.

Q: Can reports be reviewed in a study session first so there is more ease in the give-and-take between board and staff? Then the business meeting could be the executive summary and formal vote.

A: This is a good process for many boards. Members often feel freer to ask questions and achieve full understanding of the operation and level of compliance.

Q: Do OE reports add any real value to the staff or the organization?

A: As one CEO of a billion-dollar organization told us, OE reports require him to deliberately and proactively examine every aspect of the organization at least annually. The process of opening up everything to verify that all decisions are made in compliance with a stated value system allows him to have systemic and systematic knowledge, making corrections to problems that otherwise would not have been diagnosed until there was trouble. OE policies are operating standards for every facet of organizational activity. If they are viewed as such, they can be of enormous value to the organization and the people whose jobs are to make things work well.

Chapter Five

Monitoring Results Policies

The reason for any organization to exist is to provide benefits for the people it serves. Sometimes board behavior can suggest that the primary reason for the board's existence is to obsess about the facilities, or the employee compensation package, or the athletic program, or finances, or something else that has everything to do with operations. These concerns are worthy of board consideration, but they are not why the organization exists.

The issues on which boards spend most of their time, the matters that dominate their meetings, and the topics they dwell on the most, reflect the things they believe to be most important. Far too often, those things are operational in nature, as opposed to outcome focused.

To be fair, however, those operational matters are much more familiar to most board members than outcome issues are. They are much more easily discussed than whether customers and owners are getting from the organization those benefits they expect and need. Board members tend to understand (or think they do) facilities, personnel, budgets, and balance sheets based on their own professions or interests. For school boards, discussing whether all students are achieving at the levels they should is a different challenge.

Nevertheless, outcome obsession should be the hallmark of a good board. This isn't meant to suggest that efficient and effective operations are unimportant. But it is to recognize that all those operational matters mean little if the organization fails to produce the Results it exists to provide. And it is the job of the board to ensure that it does.

The board, whose members serve as trustees for the owners who themselves are not at the table or dais, often must weigh conflicting values about Results. Priorities within and among Results may need to be established to forge organizational focus. These priorities may and will shift and change as circumstances evolve, based on the actual performance of the various parts of the organization and its clients. As these shifts occur, various elements of the universe served by the organization may feel that they are being neglected or shortchanged in some way, all of which adds to the board's challenge to skillfully lead the organization.

The board's commitment is to serve, to lead, and to represent all subgroups for the ultimate health and common good of the whole. These three dimensions of board work—serving, leading, and representing—can, and at times will, come into conflict with each other. Such is the nature of board work. This dilemma is a central reason for the board to take seriously the challenge to develop and implement an effective strategic engagement plan to explain, advocate for, and gain support for Results achievement, a role we discuss in depth in Chapter 7.

In this world of governing coherently, the board determines in policy the Results to be achieved. Once the board has determined *what* must be achieved, it then delegates to the CEO and staff all decisions related to *how* the Results are to be achieved. But CEO and staff choices must be made within the decision-making parameters defined by the board in its Operational Expectations policies.

All of this works if the board is diligent in performing its critical role in this exchange: effectively monitoring Results progress. Quality Results monitoring allows the board to:

- Monitor the progress being made incrementally by the organization to achieve the board's Results; and
- Build a portfolio of CEO performance in the Results half of the CEO's job expectations.

MONITORING PROCESS

Not unexpectedly, the process for monitoring Results may follow a variety of options. As with OE monitoring, we recommend an initial two-step process:

Step 1 should include board acceptance of the CEO's interpretation of the policy, choice of indicators, baseline data, and both short-term and longer-term performance targets for each indicator.

Step 2 is the full monitoring report, including data against each indicator, an analysis of the data, and conclusions regarding progress. An assessment of reasonable progress—or not—should be asserted for each section of policy and for the policy overall.

After the first monitoring cycle, both steps can be merged into a single monitoring event, since only targets are likely to change appreciably from one monitoring cycle to another.

RESULTS MONITORING REPORT COVER SHEETS

All complete Results monitoring reports should contain a consistent set of elements in a report cover sheet that includes:

1. An initial statement from the CEO certifying to the board that the report is a true and accurate reflection of the organization's performance;
2. A certification from the CEO to the board of his or her conclusions of the organization's status of reasonable progress, based on the data collected, such that:
   - reasonable progress has been made;
   - reasonable progress has been made with the exception of identified specific performance areas; or
   - reasonable progress has not been made.
3. An executive summary that essentially says, "Here is what you will find in the report."
4. An abbreviated summary analysis of what the data told the CEO. (More detailed analyses should be presented in the subpolicy sections along with the data that have been collected.)
5. A record of the board's disposition of the report and signature of the board president with accompanying board conclusions or directions.

Figure 5.1 is a Results Monitoring Report Cover Sheet that captures each of these necessary components.

THE COMPLETE REPORT

Following these components on the cover of the report, the detailed section-by-section report continues with the following components:

- A restatement of the board's policy, section by section. Each restated policy section is followed by:
- The CEO's preapproved literal interpretation of the board's policy, as well as preapproved indicators selected by the CEO to judge reasonable progress;

(Organization Name)
Results Monitoring Document
R- (#)__ : (Title)

Certification of the CEO: *I certify this report to be accurate*

Signed: _____, CEO   Date: _____

__Approval of Interpretation and Indicators as Reasonable

    Evidence sufficient to demonstrate:

__Reasonable Progress

__Failure to Make Reasonable Progress

__Reasonable Progress with Noted Exceptions Below

_____
_____

Executive Summary:

Summative Analysis:

Disposition of the Board:

__Approve Interpretation/Indicators as Reasonable

__Reasonable Progress

__Failure to Make Reasonable Progress

__Reasonable Progress with Noted Exceptions

Summary statement/motion of the Board:

Signed: _____, President Date: _____ Re-monitor: _____

Figure 5.1. Results Monitoring Document

- Identification of the baseline and preapproved targets for each indicator;
- Presentation of data against the preapproved indicators and targets demonstrating whether the targets were achieved;
- An analysis of the data presented for each section, as appropriate; and
- A statement of conclusion about whether the data illustrate reasonable progress, or not, for the particular part of the policy being monitored.

None of these steps should be eliminated.

By preapproving the interpretation, indicators, and targets before the complete monitoring report is developed, the board sets the stage for strategic decision-making by the CEO and staff, with assurance that the board and CEO share a common understanding about the reasonableness of these critical components. This Step 1 action serves the purpose of defining what reasonable progress is, and should reduce any potential differences of opinion about whether reasonable progress has been made later when monitoring data are provided.

This final Step 2 monitoring report must be separated from the initial preliminary steps by a reasonable period of time in order to allow the CEO to gear up for the measurement of progress. The CEO and staff will use the interpretations, indicators, and performance targets previously accepted by the board as the basis for their assessment of progress. During the first year of implementation for most organizations, this second step—complete Results monitoring—usually comes a year or so following the first step.

JUDGING REASONABLE PROGRESS

Here is the tricky part for all boards: If all preapproved targets were hit, little judgment about reasonable organizational progress would be necessary; by definition, the organization's progress would be considered reasonable. But what if some, but not all, targets were hit? What if the trend line moved in the right direction, but targets were not hit? What if the overall monitoring numbers looked relatively bleak, but some external factors over which the organization had little or no control played a significant part in those Results?

For example, we have worked with one client that suffered from massive flooding in the city that disrupted every part of the organization. Another experienced a huge surge in a non-English-speaking immigrant student population in one year. Another had an abrupt and significant turnover at the senior executive staff level. Still another experienced a disruptive teachers' strike. All of these unexpected events dramatically affected both operations and Results.

Regardless of what the numbers presented by the monitoring report reveal, the board still has work to do. It will be challenged to *reasonably* use the data that are presented and weigh the Results against all known factors in order to reach a fair and reasonable assessment of organizational progress. Every effort should be made to quantify success and try to take all the possible guesswork out of the process. But in the end, reasonable people must make the best decision they can, using the best information they have, to fairly judge organizational performance.

Once the report is presented, the board must formally act by deciding from among the following choices:

- Reasonable progress has been achieved;
- Reasonable progress has been made with specified exception(s); or
- Reasonable progress has not been achieved.

The board's action should be recorded on the cover of the monitoring report (sample reports are found in Appendices C & D). Any commendations for extraordinary performance or direction for improvement should be added in the board comment section. This serves as a record of the board's disposition of the report and informs board discussion during the CEO's summative evaluation.

Board disposition of the monitoring report closes the loop on that particular monitoring event. The monitoring document and report become a part of the CEO's cumulative performance portfolio, and will be critical to the board's decision-making during the CEO summative evaluation later in the year.

A word of caution to boards as they assess organizational performance: *Improvement will not always move in a straight, upward trajectory.* It is reasonable to set targets and try diligently to meet them for every indicator every year. But our real-world experiences tell us that that will not always happen.

At any given measurement point, it is logical to expect to see more progress in some areas or more with some groups than others. And it is predictable that some indicators will show progress while others may not. What the board should look for is performance over time. The CEO's analysis and the board's consideration could include questions such as these:

- Are the trend lines moving in the right direction?
- Are there justifiable reasons for progress, or for any failure to achieve it?
- What strategies and action steps does the CEO intend to take to improve?
- What are the targets for next year, and should they be adjusted based on this year's performance?

RESULTS MONITORING GUIDELINES FOR THE CEO

Because of the high level of importance assigned to Results monitoring and the significant impact the process can have throughout the organization (as well as on the CEO's own evaluation), the CEO should take this challenge as one of the most important jobs of the CEO and key staff. We offer these words of guidance to the CEO about how to build these complete reports:

1. *Certify the accuracy of the report.* Certify to the board that the information contained in the report is true and accurate. It usually is not fatal to fail to make reasonable progress. It can be fatal to provide a report that lacks full integrity and accuracy.
2. *Provide an executive summary of what all the proceeding data reveal, including:*
   - *A clear indication of whether targets were met:* Is it reasonable to conclude that progress still was achieved, even if targets were not met?
   - *The identification of any exceptions to reasonable progress.*
3. *Following the cover page, provide a glossary of terms* to include any terminology unique to your industry, keeping in mind that board members may not understand all the lexicon of the organization.
4. *Restate the policy preamble and its approved reasonable interpretation.* Don't make the board cross-reference the policy to the report. Keep the flow of the report complete, sequential, logical, and simple.
5. *Section by section, restate the policy subpart, the approved interpretation and accompanying preapproved indicators.* Again, the intent here is to ensure the clear sequence and understanding of the report.
6. *Identify authentic and reliable indicators:* Indicators are observable behaviors, actions, or documentable Results. Sometimes assessment tools, metrics, or tests can constitute indicators. For example, an indicator of progress for a school organization may be standardized tests that measure academic performance. Indicators for other "nonacademic" Results may be less precise and more difficult to determine, but equally important.
7. *Establish a baseline current performance for each indicator.* In order to measure progress, the organization must know where it is now. The CEO must establish a baseline of current performance for each indicator to allow concrete determination about whether reasonable gain has been achieved at some point in the future. If an insurance pool board values a confidence level of 90 percent and the current level is 80 percent, progress should be measured against the 80 percent, the baseline.

8. *Set incremental targets, or goals, for each indicator.* If students are graduating at a 60 percent level at the point of baseline, and the ultimate Result policy expects 100 percent, incremental targets stretching toward 100 percent should be set and measured against longitudinally, over time. We recommend both short-term, such as one year, and longer-term targets, such as five years out.
9. *Monitor reasonable progress.* Have the targets been achieved using the indicators you selected? If so, celebrate and establish new targets. If not, why not? In instances of failure to achieve reasonable progress, the CEO should identify where the problem areas are, include any strategic changes the organization anticipates making in order to improve performance, and forecast the time needed to show improvement.
10. *Provide an appendix labeled Process at the end of the report* (optional). Now is the time to identify the strategies and actions that you believe "paid off" in contributing to success. Now that you have analyzed the data, successes, and failures, what do you intend to do about it? Potential information that might find its way into this section could include such things as increased professional development, revised schedules, new employees, etc.
11. *Provide an appendix labeled Capacity Building* (optional). If new resources are needed, if new strategies are necessary, or if different actions are required *that will currently exceed organizational capacity*, this is the place to inform the board.

SHARING STRATEGIES TO ACHIEVE INCREASED PERFORMANCE

Other than the sharing of all letters except for a "c" and "gr," the words "process" and "progress" have nothing in common. Yet, when we review Results (and even Operational Expectations) monitoring reports, it is clear that some CEOs and staff members seem to consider the two words to be almost interchangeable. Processes used by organizations far too frequently are disguised as either compliance in the case of Operational Expectations reports, or as progress in the case of Results reports.

We sometimes get so caught up in strategies and processes that we fall in love with them, and we fail to devote any attention whatsoever to whether they are producing the outcomes they are intended to produce. Winston Churchill is famously quoted as saying: "However beautiful the strategy, you should occasionally look at the results."

This is one of the most frequent criticisms we have of staff efforts to produce effective reports to the board documenting reasonable progress with

Results policies. If the CEO and staff will religiously follow the monitoring sequence we discussed earlier in this chapter, there should be no confusion about what is evidence of progress and what is process.

Yet invariably, CEOs and staff members want desperately to inform the board of all the good work they are doing, and all the great strategies and activities the organization has in place. And of course, most boards are eager to learn about all these neat things that are happening in the operational side of the organization.

In the final analysis, there is nothing wrong with the board's knowing about process. In fact, board knowledge of organizational programs and strategies can help the board perform its advocacy role in support of the organization and where it is headed.

But the question to be considered is whether the Results monitoring report is the place to share such operational information. As we discussed earlier, if monitoring data reveal that reasonable progress has not been made, the board likely expects to know what will change in order to produce better Results. So, at least in this case, strategic and programmatic information will find its way into the report.

But process information must be separated very obviously from monitoring data, and it must be called what it is: process information. The board never should be confused about the information it is using to make judgments about organizational performance. Mixing operational activities with Results performance data can have that outcome, and they must be avoided. If and when operational activity information is presented as a part of a Results monitoring report, it should be presented under a separate heading, clearly labeled as, for example, *"Program and Strategic Information: Incidental Only,"* and preferably placed at the end of the report as an appendix.

The message here: Take every precaution against inviting the board back into the world of organizational strategy. That is the world of the CEO and staff. The board has good reason to want to know about the important operational decisions that are being made. But the board now lives in the world of governance, not operations. The CEO must take care not to lead the board into the staff's domain, or confuse the role clarity that Coherent Governance achieves.

SOME ADDITIONAL SUGGESTIONS FOR THE CEO

When presenting Results monitoring reports to the board, the CEO should:

1. Provide organization-wide aggregated performance data based on all monitoring indicators previously accepted by the board. Supplement this

information with disaggregated data, depending on the specific subgroups served by your organization.
2. To the extent possible, include data illustrating progress over time. Longitudinal charts are helpful and meet the increasing desire of most boards to see performance trends from year to year.
3. In the analysis: List conclusions to be drawn from the data. Note strengths as well as weaknesses. When significant, describe and explain performance differences among subgroups, as well as any organizational failure to hit performance targets. Note any concerns about the validity or reliability of the data and its application to the specifics of the clients the organization serves.
4. If there is a large amount of information to be considered, spread the presentation across two or more board meetings.
5. Be sure the text is "digestible": concise, understandable, and supplemented by clear graphics.

The CEO logically will delegate the development of monitoring reports to the staff member(s) who have the greatest level of responsibility in specific Results areas. Nevertheless, vetting these reports through the senior staff or administrative cabinet provides opportunities to refine the reports before they go to the board.

Included on the following page is a sample staff assignment and report development timeline created by one school superintendent.

RECEIVING AND DISPOSING OF REPORTS

The art of receiving and responding to reports is not magical, but it is important. Remember, by the time a report gets to the board, the CEO and staff now have invested considerable time and effort in building a document they believe fairly represents the organization's performance. The reports and staff members who prepared them deserve due consideration within the framework of what the board is there to decide.

Both the CEO and the board president should establish a clear context for receiving a report and what is expected from the board. What is the board being asked to do? Is the board being asked to accept the interpretation and indicators as reasonable? Approve the proposed targets as reasonable? Accept and judge the evidence of reasonable progress? The task should be clearly understood.

Following is a sample introductory statement that clarifies for the board, staff, and audience exactly what the report is intended to accomplish:

Exhibit 5.1. Sample Results Report Prep Schedule

RESULT	Point Person	Draft to Cabinet	Final to Cabinet	Report to CEO Secretary	Report Sent to the Board	Board Meeting
1 Mission (M)	CEO					Mon
2 Literacy (I)						June 30
2 Numeracy (I)		Mon July 2	Fri July 6	Mon July 16	Mon July 23	Mon July 30
2 Technology (I)		Thurs July 12	Fri July 19	Mon July 30	Fri Aug 10	Wed August 27
2 Academic Performance (M)		Mon Sept 3	Fri Sept 7	Wed Sept 12	Fri Sept 17	Mon September 24
4 Character (I)						
3 Citizenship (I)						
2 Science (I)		Tues Oct 2	Tues Oct 9	Wed Oct 17	Mon Oct 22	Mon October 29
6 Balanced and Healthy Lives (I)						
2 Social Studies (I)		Wed Oct 26	Tues Oct 31	Mon Nov 12	Fri Nov 16	Mon November 26
2 Visual and Performing Arts (I)		Mon Nov 19	Fri Nov 23	Mon Dec 3	Fri Dec 7	Mon December 17
3 Citizenship (M)		Fri Dec 14	Fri Dec 21	Mon Jan 14	Fri Jan 18	Mon January 26
2 World Languages (I)						
6 Balanced and Healthy Lives (M)		Wed Jan 23	Mon Jan 28	Mon Feb 11	Fri Feb 15	Mon February 25
2 Health/PE (I)						
4 Character (M)		Wed Feb 20	Mon Feb 25	Mon Mar 11	Fri Mar 15	Mon March 25
No Report						April
5 Workplace Performance (M)		Wed May 1	Fri May 6	Mon May 13	Fri May 17	Mon May 27

Notes:
RI = Reasonable Interpretation
I = Indicators
B = Baseline
T = Targets
M = Monitoring Reasonable Progress
- senior staff assigned by CEO
- consultant review returned to point person after final cabinet review within twenty-four hours
- reports due to board on Fridays, approximately two weeks prior to board meeting

SAMPLE: PRESIDENT'S STATEMENT TO OPEN DISCUSSION ON A RESULTS REPORT

"Members of the board have received and reviewed the CEO's (reasonable interpretation) or (monitoring) report on R-____. It now is the board's responsibility to consider the reasonableness of this interpretation, including the choice of indicators and targets (and the data presented to document performance), and to judge reasonable progress in this Results area.

"Following the CEO's overview of the report, I will invite any member of the board who has questions or comments about the report to offer them to the CEO or his designee. Let me remind the board that the criteria for judging the report are whether the board is satisfied that:

1. the policy and its subparts have been reasonably interpreted, whether the CEO has selected reasonable indicators and set reasonable performance targets; and
2. the data illustrate whether the organization has made reasonable progress in this Results area.

"I encourage members to limit their questions and comments to these criteria."

RECEIVING THE REPORT

After the president has "teed up" the report, the CEO then is expected to either present an overview of the report or introduce a key member of the staff to do so. The task of the point person who assumes that responsibility is not to read the report, but to offer a brief summary of the highlights and the conclusions. The person who presents this verbal executive summary should anticipate the board's questions and concerns, depending on the Results that have been achieved, and provide answers to questions as well as they can be anticipated. Any further clarity about what is expected of the board should be discussed, as well.

After this staff summary of the report, the board should be invited to pose any questions to the CEO or key staff member. *At this stage, the report still is the property of the CEO.* Members of the board should take advantage of this opportunity to question the CEO in order to ensure full understanding of the report and the data and conclusions the CEO and staff have reached about performance.

BOARD PROCESS TO JUDGE THE REPORT

Following the Q&A discussion, the next action that should be taken is the president's call for a motion to accept the report as presented. *Once that motion is made, ownership of the report is transferred from the CEO to the board.* Since the report now belongs to the board, any discussion about it should be among members of the board only. Beginning the discussion with a formal motion helps focus the conversation on the question. It minimizes the board's temptation to wander around in various aspects of the report or become distracted by other extraneous issues that have little to do with the board's task: to judge reasonable progress.

We recommend starting the process with a "clean" motion to accept the report as presented, even if members of the board have issues with certain parts of it. Those concerns may be expressed via the amendment process after deliberation begins. To try to start the board's discussion with a motion that includes both acceptance of the report and exceptions to it confuses the board's conversation—and it is inconsistent with accepted parliamentary procedure.

Of course, if the board is convinced that the report simply isn't ready for prime time, an opening motion could be made to postpone consideration until a later date or some such motion. Normally, however, if the board is prepared to receive and act on the report, the simple *motion to accept and approve* will start that discussion very effectively.

Following is a sample motion to be used to accept the report and to begin the process of deliberation, using standard parliamentary procedure:

SAMPLE MOTION TO INITIATE CONSIDERATION OF RESULTS MONITORING REPORTS

1. *Initial motion:*

"Mr./Madam President, I move that the board accept and approve the CEO's monitoring report on R__ as presented."
Second, then discuss and vote.

2. *Possible amending motion* **(offered by an individual member who disagrees with the reasonableness of the CEO's interpretation, indicators, targets, or assertion of reasonable progress):**

"Mr./Madam President, I move to amend the motion by _____."
Second, then discuss and vote.

Appendices C and D include two sample partial Results reports.

JUDGING: ORGANIZATIONAL OR CEO PERFORMANCE?

As was the case with OE monitoring, what the board is doing when it acts on a Results monitoring report is expressing its satisfaction—or lack thereof—with the *organization's* performance.

Since the board's policy states that the organization's performance and the CEO's performance are identical, then, of course, both technically are being evaluated simultaneously. However, the starting point for the board's Results monitoring is a review of the organization's performance, knowing that at some point in the future the CEO will be credited with the results of that action. This initial focus on organizational performance prevents the evaluation of the CEO at every meeting. The CEO's personal evaluation usually will occur in closed session when the summative evaluation is conducted. Chapter 6 discusses this CEO evaluation topic in greater depth.

QUESTIONS FOR THOUGHT

1. How does your board now judge whether your organization is succeeding in meeting its outcome expectations?
2. What percentage of its time does your board now spend doing that work?
3. Would your board and CEO agree that progress toward achieving Results should be the dominant expectation of the board and the primary obligation of the CEO?

FAQS

Q: Whose job is it to schedule the monitoring of Results?

A: The board's. That said, the schedule—or annual work plan—would be developed in concert with the CEO as consideration is given to available and relevant data. Priority Results may be identified and take first place on the calendar. Caution should be exercised in delaying attention to other Results for too long. Results ultimately are intimately interconnected in achieving the mission. At minimum, the reasonable interpretation for each Result should be approved by the board during the first year.

Q: How do you recognize when Results are driving the organization and all staff efforts, signaling to the board that systemic and systematic alignment has been realized?

A: Actually, this becomes quite evident rather quickly. Are the Results published internally and externally? Do site leaders talk about OE and Results with their line staff? Are staff evaluations aligned to achieving Results? Do staff members understand the alignment of their accountability with the CEOs? Are Results policies visible in buildings, the boardroom, and offices? If questioned, would clients/customers/members/students know what the Results are?

Q: If the board decides that the report failed to demonstrate reasonable progress in one area, does that automatically throw the entire report into "unreasonable progress" status?

A: No. The board must apply the reasonable person standard and judge how significant the exception to the whole is. If the board concludes that every part of the Results policy is shown to be making reasonable progress with one exception, the overall assessment of progress would be "reasonable progress with the exception of . . ."

Chapter Six

Evaluating the CEO in This New Governing Environment

> *The Board considers CEO performance to be identical to organizational performance. Organizational accomplishment of the Board's Results policies and operation according to the values expressed in the Board's Operational Expectations policies will be considered successful CEO performance. These two components define the CEO's job responsibilities, and are the basis for the CEO's performance evaluation. (Coherent Governance Policy Template BCR-5)*

The above policy statement is extracted from Coherent Governance templates, and it is very consistent with policy language found in most Policy Governance manuals. It represents one of the fundamental and most significant concepts of both models: The performance of the organization and the performance of the CEO are identical. Stated simply, as goes the organization, so goes the CEO.

The previous two chapters in this book dealt with the board's monitoring role for both Operational Expectations and Results policies. As we will see in Chapter 8, the board will develop an annual work plan that schedules the formal monitoring of the policies in these two categories throughout the year. As the board monitors R & OE policies, it is making judgments about the organization's reasonable progress toward achieving the Results, and its satisfaction with the organization's operational compliance with the standards set by the OE policies.

As the board makes these judgments about the organization's performance, it also is building a portfolio of CEO performance. At the end of the complete monitoring cycle, these judgments of organizational performance will be "transferred" to the CEO, which serves to link the two together—as the above policy suggests.

This process is a dramatic departure from the methods most boards use to evaluate their CEOs. As a result of our combined seventy-plus years of working with boards, one startling fact has become clear: Most boards have no idea how to meaningfully evaluate their CEOs. From our experience, let us share the norm, rather than the exception, about how boards approach the process.

At the eleventh hour, a board president may call for help in a scramble to find a generic evaluation document to use for the CEO's evaluation, with no forethought about what that evaluation is intended to measure. During CEO evaluation discussion sessions, members might contribute their personal feelings, biases, and reactions to how the CEO handled the latest challenge—or perhaps mishandled it, coloring a year's worth of work. Often the information discussed and documented as "evaluative" has little or no connection to the CEO's or the organization's actual performance.

As individual board members struggle with how to approach the task of CEO evaluation, they sometimes voice opinions ranging from *"no one deserves all A's"* to *"an evaluation isn't the time to criticize—look how hard s/he has been working."* This retrospective would be remiss if it didn't also include reference to evaluations characterized by such personal attitudes ranging from *"the CEO can do no wrong,"* to the opposite, *"the CEO can do nothing right."*

Quite obviously, neither mind-set is commendable. Many times, given the difficulty of conducting evaluations that all parties find meaningful, boards skip the process altogether.

A MEANINGFUL EVALUATION PROCESS

The concept of linking organizational performance with CEO performance, as defined in the Results and Operational Expectations policies, means that if the organization's owners and clients realize the benefits the board said they should, and if the organization operates within the values of the board's Operational Expectations policies, the CEO has done the job he or she was hired to do.

If the board means what it has said in policy, these are the only criteria on which the CEO will be evaluated.

Actually, the process of CEO evaluation no longer is a one-time event, but rather an ongoing, continuous process. Each time the board monitors one of the Results or the OE policies, it is building a portion of the CEO's annual performance evaluation. The board is, in fact, creating a performance portfolio that at a defined point later in the year will become the basis for the CEO's summative evaluation.

When the scheduled time for the summative evaluation arrives on the board's annual work plan, the compilation of board judgments on each report is reviewed. Let us point out here the invaluable role to be played by an assistant to the board who compiles each monitoring report and maintains records of board action to be used for this summative evaluation purpose.

We also should re-emphasize here the extreme importance of using a well-designed cover sheet for each monitoring report (see Chapters 4 and 5 for examples of good monitoring report covers), and the value of accurate and consistent recording of board action on each report. At the end of the annual monitoring cycle, when all these OE & R reports are pulled and reviewed as the basis for the CEO's summative evaluation, it will become clear why we emphasize this point. The board will not want to review—again—a full year of complete monitoring reports to refresh its thinking about how it disposed of each report. Well-designed cover sheets that reflect the board's actions and comments at the time of monitoring will be invaluable time-savers (and faithful records) when the summative evaluation is being conducted. We have facilitated summative evaluations that had the advantage of such well-designed cover sheets in three hours or less, and we have spent more than a full day doing the same thing when there were no such cover sheets to rely upon.

Based upon the monitoring record compiled throughout the year, the board president or a trusted coach facilitates the board discussion and drafts a summary evaluation document of that discussion for board approval. The board's summative evaluation of the CEO could be no more than two or three pages of narrative comment, all based on the record generated by ongoing Results and Operational Expectations monitoring.

This illustrates why the OE & R monitoring process is so crucial to the overall effectiveness of the board's movement into Coherent Governance. If the board fails to do this job very well, it has, in fact, given away control of the organization. But if the board performs the monitoring role efficiently and effectively, it assumes a far greater degree of control than any "traditional" governing method would permit. And it assigns a greater degree of accountability than it ever thought possible.

Let us repeat here that from a technical standpoint, the regular and systematic monitoring of the Results and Operational Expectations policies at board meetings are occasions for the board to assess how well the *organization*—not the CEO—is performing. At the point of the summative evaluation of the CEO, this record of organizational performance is transferred to the CEO, at which time the monitoring Results become personal, not organizational. This subtle but important distinction prevents the CEO's evaluation at regular—and sometimes public—meetings.

Let us emphasize an important point about the board's summarizing the year's monitoring decisions. If the board has anything to say about exceptional organizational performance, good or bad, the time to say it is when the relevant policy is being monitored. If the board has gone through a full year of monitoring the Results and Operational Expectations policies and has said nothing about a particular concern, it is unfair to inject any such unstated concerns during the summative CEO evaluation process.

The purpose of the summative evaluation is to *summarize*, to draw conclusions from the work that has been done during the complete R & OE monitoring cycle.

If the board has concerns about the maintenance of its facilities, for example, it should make a compliance judgment when the facilities OE policy is monitored, not inject such a concern after the fact. On the other side of that same coin, if the board recognizes extraordinary performance and feels it appropriate to offer commendation for it, that decision should be made when the relevant policy is monitored.

After the board has disposed of a monitoring report, the president might ask if the board has any specific feedback to offer, either positive or negative. It is here that board direction or commendation might be offered by the board, but only if a proper motion is made and approved. Remember, the board acts only when it officially votes, so group sharing of individual ideas is nothing more than that.

Of course, CEOs tend to accept, with gratitude, commendation whenever and however it is offered, whether the board made such a formal decision when the policy was being monitored or not. Nevertheless, in order to build a system that is based on consistency and reliability, the board should develop the habit of assessing organizational performance very thoroughly and fairly when it is time to do so. Then, the board uses the record of its actions as the complete basis for summative CEO evaluation.

The summative review is a look back in history. As the board does this review, it should look for trends as well as for aberrations. As we have facilitated these summative evaluations with boards over the years, three occasions of trends that were identified and that influenced the evaluation come to mind as examples to learn from:

1. The CEO's communication deficits were confirmed when the board reviewed its responses to OE policies on Communication with the Owners and Communication with the Board. Based on the board's summative judgment that the CEO clearly had communication issues, the board required professional development for the CEO to improve her skills.

2. Another board's overall concerns about financial management were confirmed when it reviewed its past action in response to the three monitoring reports dealing with money and assets—budget, financial administration, and asset protection. All three reflected similar concerns. The CEO's summative evaluation highlighted these board concerns and identified this area of organizational performance as a priority for improvement over the next year.
3. Another board prioritized the lack of reasonable progress in one Result area based on a consistent pattern of underperformance for the previous three years. That multi-year record compiled through the Results policy monitoring process was clear demonstration that the pattern of poor performance was not improving. The board's choice to continue to accept this failure came to an end. The summative evaluation was worded quite strongly: "We expect performance to improve during the coming year. Further failure to achieve reasonable progress will not be acceptable to the board or to our community." Exhibit 6.1 is the evaluation summary of a very high-performing school district CEO. It is thorough and clear. Note that it addresses commendations to the CEO, areas of performance in which the board wants to see improvement, and what the board itself commits to contribute to that improvement. For obvious reasons, we have omitted any identifying information.

Exhibit 6.2 provides a sample of another CEO evaluation. It is far shorter and does not refer to any detailed statements of condition about each OE or Results policy in the chart. This sample is from a board that meets quarterly.

QUESTIONS FOR THOUGHT

1. How does your board now conduct CEO evaluations?
2. Are they based on a well-defined set of expectations that includes both operational and Results performance?
3. Does your board now make decisions—through the approval process or otherwise—for which the CEO ultimately is held accountable?

EXHIBIT 6.1.
SUMMATIVE SUPERINTENDENT EVALUATION

TO: Superintendent
FR: Board of Education
RE: Superintendent Evaluation

The ____ Board of Education met Saturday, April 8, to review your performance as Superintendent during the previous year. The Board appreciated the strength of your leadership, which is blended with obvious empathy and support for students.

Among your many strengths and positive attributes are: your visibility in, and relationship with, the community; your support of the Board and its role relationship with you and the staff; your willingness to take reasoned risk in pursuit of progress (IB, personalized learning); your support for cutting-edge innovations; your approachable style and your commitment to self-improvement (such as Broad Academy, AASA Leadership Academy). You have made excellent employment choices and have taken steps to improve site leadership performance.

While student achievement always will be a moving target, the Board appreciates your commitment to make increased performance levels the centerpiece of your focus.

Let us say again, all five of us are pleased with your leadership, your understanding and proactive support of our governance role, and the path we are taking together in focusing on students and their achievement.

You are tireless, positive, solution oriented, unerringly focused on students, a person rightfully growing in local, state and national recognition for your skills, your courage and your professionalism. You have our thanks, our support and our esteem, and we look forward to a long and productive relationship working for the success of all our students.

_____   _____
president   vice-president

_____   _____
secretary   treasurer

_____
director

Operational Expectations Performance Summary

In reviewing all of the Operational Expectations, our focus is prioritized on further increasing the quality and extent of communication between us as a board and with you as individual members to forge our relationships, support and understanding.

All report covers must include the certification of the superintendent as to compliance and an overall analysis on the cover sheet to summarize and memorialize your analysis—what you have learned from the data collection.

OE.1: Global Operational Expectation
Monitored only the Reasonable Interpretation since more detailed monitoring of this policy's values is reflected in the monitoring of all OE reports, 2–13.

OE.2: Emergency Superintendent Succession
The Board accepted this report as compliant. The Board requests that emergency successors are listed by name rather than position.

The Board has concerns about a broader succession plan for the District, but it recognizes that OE.2 is limited to emergency conditions, not long-term succession planning. To follow up, the Board needs to identify its concerns about longer-term criteria and succession in additional policy for the sake of the district.

OE.3: Treatment of Stakeholders
The fact that only 60 percent of the staff responded favorably to a question about stakeholder input (OE-3.3), rather than the 80 percent indicator, provides room for improvement. Overall, however, the Board continues to recognize the strong gains being made in building a very favorable district culture. Your visibility throughout the community has served the district well.

To follow-up, the Board will revisit the wording of this policy to remove "staff" and keep this policy focused solely on external stakeholders. This will change next year's interpretation and indicators. Our concerns about staff will be addressed in OE.4.8.

OE.4 Personnel Administration
The most recent OE-4 report fails to include a "Certification of Compliance" from the Superintendent informing the Board of the Superintendent's judgment of district performance. This section of the cover sheet always should be included in the reports. The Board may table future reports if they fail to include this important provision.

You continue to demonstrate exceptional skill in dealing effectively with challenging staff issues. There seems to be a high level of mutual trust between the Superintendent and staff.

The Board appreciates the gains being made in teacher retention, even though the numerical target in 4.8 was not achieved. Since the performance target was not achieved, the Board assumes the same target will be retained for next year. You have clearly done a good job in addressing retention.

(continued)

EXHIBIT 6.1. *(Continued)*

OE.5 Learning Environment
Although the district's performance for one of the learning environment indicators fell slightly below the numerical target (85% v 83%), the Board nevertheless believes that the overall learning environment of the district contributes in a significant way to increased student academic performance.

OE.6 Financial Planning
The Board remains very confident about the overall financial management of the district. We appreciate the gains that have been made in updating the district's financial management systems to assure the highest level of effective stewardship of our resources.

OE.7 Financial Administration
Full compliance is noted. The Board, as pointed out in OE-6, maintains high confidence in the district's performance.

OE.8 Asset Protection
There is continued strong performance in the protection of the district's assets.

The Board notes that all three OE policies dealing with the district's resources (OE-6, OE-7 and OE-8) are regarded as fully compliant and being managed at an exceptionally high level. The Board is able to focus most of its time and attention on matters dealing with students and their progress because of its high level of confidence in the way money and assets are being managed and protected.

OE.9 Communicating with the Board
Although we believe the level and nature of communication between the Superintendent and Board is strong and effective, there are opportunities to improve the flow of information. Our goal would be to assure full and timely Board knowledge and understanding of matters in order to effectively support the district and respond to public inquiries. Sections 9.4 and 9.5 especially note the Board's expectations in this area. The Board recognizes that operation of the district is the responsibility of the Superintendent (the Board has no interest in assuming any part of that role). Nevertheless, we believe we should be "in the loop" as much as possible in matters of district importance. The Board reiterates the values expressed in OE-9.11 concerning advance notification of significant changes to the instructional program. The Board needs to be informed and understand any such proposed changes in sufficient time to provide any related feedback to the Superintendent and again, to respond to public comment.

The Board understands that the Superintendent may select the communication devices he believes best to keep the Board informed. However, we will schedule time for an informal conversation about means for routinely informing the Board of significant district concerns (OE-9 preamble).

OE.10 Communicating with the Public
The Board appreciates the efforts you have made and directed to communicate effectively with the public. A continuing concern, one that has persisted for a number of years, relates to the visibility of the Board in its role as elected leaders governing the district. The Board itself has limited opportunities to maintain visibility with the citizens who elected its members. While no member of the Board wants visibility and recognition simply for the sake of being visible and recognized, the Board believes the public should be reminded often of the Board's trustee role. District efforts must be made to support Board communication/engagement, and to embrace every reasonable opportunity to include the Board in presentations, publications and events.

* The Board will consider appropriate policy language to assure that its concern re: staff support for communication in OE.10 is reflected in policy, which then will be monitored.

OE.11 Instructional Program
Although certain performance targets were not achieved, the Board considers the overall instructional program to be operating at a high level. The Board recognizes that the performance targets were set quite high, as they should be, and that actual performance was very close to target.

Reporting of district performance must include an executive summary and overall analysis, informing the Board of overall conclusions reached by staff as a result of the data resulting from monitoring.

OE.12 Discipline
The Board is pleased that the restorative justice program was expanded.

OE.13 Facilities
Performance in this monitoring report remains well documented, straightforward and clear.

Results Performance Summary

In reviewing all Results, we want to reaffirm our deepest belief that reading should continue to be the district's priority. It is fundamental to all other learning.

R-1 Reading:
The overall judgment of Reading performance is, as certified by you, failing to make reasonable progress. However, the Board recognizes that the recent report represented the first monitoring event following baseline, and that the district is in the early stages of effectively monitoring this discipline. The Board is pleased with the initial selection of indicators, the attention being paid to the achievement gap, and the overall direction being taken.

Given the overall level of reading performance, the Board is interested in learning more about the strategies being taken to improve reading performance.

(continued)

EXHIBIT 6.1. *(Continued)*

There is little Board interest in comparing our district's student performance against the state and general averages. The Board believes there is greater value in using cohort data rather than comparison with other districts or the state. The Board is interested in exploring with the Superintendent the question of validity (one state assessment) as an indicator of student performance.

The monitoring of (state assessment), we believe, is an indicator of ELL achievement related to reading and writing and should be placed there appropriately and not monitored as a Result.

R-1 Other Disciplines:
The Board is anticipating receiving initial monitoring reports on the other R-1 disciplines during this calendar year and prior to the next summative evaluation. (Note: the Board will schedule a conversation about monitoring certain aspects of Social Studies as a part of the focus on R-3, as opposed to monitoring it as a separate and new discipline of R-1.)

R-2 and R-3:
The Board has delayed the monitoring of R-2 and R-3. We have calendared the consideration of the reasonable interpretation and indicators for R-2 for September and R-3 in December.

Exhitit 6.1:
Summary resolutions for the coming year

The Board has renumbered its Results policies, beginning with the Mission listed as R-1, followed by R-2 Academics, etc. The primary reason for this change is to permit the Mission to be monitored as R-1, allowing graduation rates, AP enrollment and concurrent enrollment to be used as monitoring indicators for the Mission. These outcomes are being monitored now, but not specifically related to any of the other Results.

The Board will schedule a discussion with the Superintendent about modifications to the Results monitoring process to allow overall judgments to be made about student progress by discipline, rather than by indicators.

Reporting progress by indicator is valuable, but the Board is interested in utilizing a combination of results from applicable indicators to help reach an overall judgment of performance—<u>by discipline</u>.

The Board would value receiving, as a part of every OE and Results monitoring report, an Overall Analysis of the data that have been collected for that specific report and the meaning of that data. How does this information better inform administration? Taken as a whole, what does it mean for the health of the organization? What picture does it give you and us of student achievement in each Result discipline?

Results:
Following presentation of the data and the judgment of reasonable progress, the Board would value understanding any strategic or programmatic changes the Superintendent wishes to undertake in order to improve performance. The reason is not to approve or pass judgment on any of these choices, but rather to help the Board understand your thinking and process in order to support these directions.

Operational Expectations:
Again, following presentation of the data and the judgment of compliance, the Board values understanding any strategic or programmatic changes the Superintendent wishes to undertake in order to achieve compliance. The reason is not to approve or pass judgment on any of these choices, but rather to help the Board understand your thinking and process in order to support these directions.

Applicable to reports on Results and Operational Expectations:
Improvements staff intends to initiate should be outlined in an Appendix to each report–labeled "Process"–to engender understanding and support.

Exhibit 6.1:
Further Board Work as a Result of This process

Through the process of conducting this evaluation, the board has self-reflected as well and deems it appropriate to address the following:

1. The Board has concerns about a broader succession plan for the District, but it recognizes that OE.2 is limited to emergency conditions, not long-term succession planning. To follow up, the Board needs to identify its concerns about longer-term criteria and succession in additional policy for the sake of the district.
2. To follow-up, the Board will revisit the wording of this policy, OE.3, to remove "staff" and keep this policy focused solely on external stakeholders. This will change next year's interpretation and indicators. Our concerns about staff will be addressed in OE.4.8.
3. The Board understands that the Superintendent may select the communication devices he believes best to keep the Board informed. However, we will schedule time for an informal conversation with the Superintendent about means for routinely informing the Board of significant district concerns (OE-9 preamble).
4. The Board will consider appropriate policy language to assure that its concern re: staff support for communication in OE.10 is reflected in policy, which then will be monitored.

EXHIBIT 6.2.
ANNUAL CEO SUMMATIVE EVALUATION

The purpose of the annual evaluation of the CEO is to summarize the actions previously taken by the Board as it monitored Results and Operational Expectations policies during the year, and to draw conclusions on that basis.

Board Policy BC/R-5 CEO Accountability states that the Board considers CEO performance to be identical to organizational performance. Organizational accomplishment of the Board's Results policies and operation according to the values expressed in the Board's Operational Expectations policies are considered successful CEO performance. These two components define the CEO's job responsibilities, and they are the basis for the CEO's performance evaluation.

Operational Expectations Policy		Date Monitored	Board Disposition
OE-1	Global Operational Expectation	11/17	Compliance
OE-2	Emergency CEO Succession	11/17	Compliance
OE-3	Treatment of Members	11/17	Compliance
OE-4	Personnel Administration	11/17	Compliance
OE-5	Financial Planning	2/22	Compliance
OE-6	Financial Administration	2/22	Compliance
OE-7	Asset Protection	2/22	Compliance
OE-8	Communicating with the Board	8/22	Compliance
OE-9	Coverage	8/22	Compliance
OE-10	Communicating with Members	8/22	Compliance

Results Policies		Date Monitored	Board Disposition
R-1	Mega Result	2/22	Reasonable progress has been achieved.
R-2	Rates	8/22	Reasonable progress has been achieved.
R-3	Claims Administration	11/17	Reasonable progress has been achieved.
R-4	Coverage	8/22	Reasonable progress has been achieved.
R-5	Stability and Confidence	2/22	Reasonable progress has been achieved.

Based upon the Board's prior monitoring of these policies and the ongoing monitoring of the organization's and the CEO's performance during the preceding year, the Board reaches the following summary conclusions relative to CEO performance:
The following priorities established for this year were achieved:

- Rate stabilization for members
- Advocacy with our legislators to benefit the Pool
- Completed succession plan

Based upon the foregoing conclusions, the Board determines the following: The CEO has met the expectations of the Board for PY 20__ and made adequate progress on the Results.

Based upon the foregoing conclusions, the Board establishes the following priorities for the coming year:

- Revisit the targets for Results Policies 3 & 4 "Claims Administration" and "Coverage" for relevancy and bring back recommendations that are more appropriate.
- Re-monitor OE-7 Asset Protection to include our new policy subpart on maximizing value and revenue of our property, which includes the office building.

FAQS

Q: Is it advisable to conduct a board self-assessment prior to conducting the CEO's summative evaluation?

A: Absolutely! Has the board lived up to its commitments, those expressed in the GC and BCR policies? Many of them affect the CEO's job. The board must do its job well before attempting to assess CEO performance against board expectations. Quality assessment of the performance of the board and of the CEO should travel together.

Q: Does a summative evaluation of the CEO have any real meaning? If the board has been doing its job of OE & R monitoring throughout the year, isn't this just an arcane formality?

A: The summative CEO evaluation allows the board to draw summary judgment based on the record created by Results and Operational Expectations monitoring. As a result of the year's monitoring experience, what becomes clear to the board? What performance areas are worthy of commendation? What areas become apparent as priorities for the next operational cycle? What noteworthy successes should drive decisions about performance-based compensation? The summative evaluation is the vehicle the board uses to transfer judgments of district performance to the CEO personally. It cannot be neglected.

Q: Should the CEO provide a summary self-assessment?

A: Such a self-assessment by the CEO can be useful, but it should not be substituted for the board's own deliberations and judgments, based upon the performance record that has been compiled throughout the monitoring period.

Chapter Seven

Engagement

If you are a publicly elected board member, chances are good that you engaged fairly effectively with your ownership when you campaigned for election. Or even after the election, the board very likely talked with the owners when it needed votes for new taxes or support for some other matter important to the organization.

But absent the urgent need for votes, how closely linked is the board to the people who own the organization? How proactively does the board seek continuing, meaningful dialogue with those owners?

If your board serves a membership, you probably talk with your members frequently about their concerns and about what the organization is doing on their behalf. If you have an annual conference or convention, there likely are many random conversations—"shoptalk"—during that compressed time frame.

But here is the question: When does your board, as a governing entity, deliberately communicate with its owners about matters of serious concern to the board, or about the expectations those owners have of their organization?

Once members are in office, how does the board as a single unit connect with the people those members serve, lead, and represent—not just as individuals, but as the whole board? In particular, how does the board define its governing obligation to understand and serve *all* the owners, not just a particular subpart of the ownership that may have a specific issue at the time?

In the board's new job description (GC-3), one of the first roles is the board's commitment to ongoing, proactive engagement with the owners and stakeholders. This means that the board must develop a very deliberate, structured plan for establishing and executing that kind of communication and relationship building.

Throughout this chapter, we will refer to this role as *engagement*—the practice of speaking and listening well with the hope of building ongoing and mutually supportive relationships. Some boards label the effort *linkage*, or *dialogue, community conversations, owner engagement*, or some other term. We will use *engagement* as a term that captures the role, realizing that your board may attach a different label to it.

It should be emphasized that the engagement role is a *board* responsibility, not a board *member* responsibility. Individual members have and will continue to have personal relationships with people both inside and outside the organization. But this is not *engagement* as defined in board policy. The engagement function is a whole-board function, based on strategies defined by the board. This does not necessarily mean that every member must participate in every engagement session, as we will discuss later in this chapter. It does mean that fulfillment of the board's engagement role, as defined in policy, is not an individual responsibility.

ENGAGE WITH WHOM?

A very important point needs to be made here. Some consultants and writers believe it is the board's obligation to engage only their owners, not those who have different "stakeholder" roles with the organization. Of course, depending on the type of organization the board serves, those could be, at least in large measure, the same people. In a voluntary membership organization, for example, the owners and clients virtually are the same people, although some segments of the ownership can take on a narrower client role when they have a particular need or desire not shared by the entire ownership.

It is our belief that boards owe singular loyalty to their owners—the public, in the case of a publicly elected board; or the members, in the case of a membership organization—but they can benefit from structured engagement with groups other than their owners. They can build stronger understanding of and advocacy for the organization if they develop relationships with clients and customers, for example, and with a range of stakeholder groups that have varying relationships with the organization. Examples of such other groups might be legislators, civic or philanthropic groups, law enforcement or security agencies, church leaders, or other influential groups in the community.

In the case of public school boards, engagements could be with students, the school board's clients, for example. It is not uncommon for school boards to engage with recent graduates to ask questions about their level of preparation for college or work; to explore their reflections about the school learning environment and their education experience; and to solicit their feedback about the board's Results for student achievement and their validity.

The primary objective of the engagements is to provide a means for the board to better understand the needs and expectations of the owners and those clients it serves. A second objective is to allow the board to share with the owners and stakeholders its vision for organizational performance as a means to build understanding and stronger support, and perhaps partnerships, for where the organization is headed. Our belief is that collaboration builds a better future for each partner.

The challenge to build an effective engagement plan for the board can seem formidable. If the organization is substantially "self-contained" (a volunteer membership organization, for example), meaningful engagement with the membership may be a relatively easy thing to do. But if the organization is a public school district, whose owners include everyone who lives within the borders of the district, the task is considerably more difficult.

But regardless of the nature of the organization's ownership, effectively performing this role is critical if the board is to:

- Build mutually supportive relationships between the board and its owners and stakeholders;
- Inform the board about the expectations of the owners;
- Translate the owners' expectations into policies; and
- Create understanding among the ownership about the board's Results.

SO, HOW DOES A BOARD CREATE AN ENGAGEMENT PLAN?

There are multiple ways for boards to develop a plan for communicating with or engaging their owners. A number of variables must be considered, including the size and complexity of the organization and its ownership; the nature of the organization in terms of its mission and the definition of its overall purpose; and the capacity of the organization and the board to try some sophisticated processes.

Some fundamental engagement concepts do apply to all organizations, however.

For the first engagement sessions, we recommend focusing all of your efforts on Results. *Walk the talk* about the purpose of the organization with a laser focus on the benefits to be realized by those your organization exists to serve.

We suggested in Chapter 2 that the board's early implementation of Coherent Governance should be launched with as little fanfare as possible in order to avoid making your new venture a target. Some of what we suggest here may sound contradictory, but it need not be.

There may be critical individuals and groups of your organization's owners and stakeholders who will need to understand your shift of focus in order for them to become advocates for your venture. Bring them into the loop early by establishing solid, two-way discussions with them.

Once you have adopted your policies and revised your board meeting agendas to redirect the board's dominant attention to Results, consider some of the following strategies. They are designed to focus staff and the owners, with the board, on increased achievement of Results. The list includes a variety of options to consider, based on the type of organization your board leads.

Invite targeted groups of the ownership to meet with the board. People learn by doing and engaging. You have the opportunity to brief them about the board's renewed focus on Results. You can express your need to involve and partner with them to deliver Results—to your mutual benefit.

Consider meeting with the local newspaper editorial staff. If you are a public organization, talk with local media about your new focus. Ask them to watch for the increased focus your board and organization will be demonstrating on the Results. Invite them to attend a board meeting where you are working on a Results policy.

Meet with your clients. We recommend representative discussions across the spectrum of groups served by your organization. If you are in the business of elder care, talk with your seniors and their family members. If you are a school district, student groups are enlightening—and refreshing—in their honesty. If you are an insurance pool, pool participants will have an avid interest in your identified Results. The members of a voluntary membership organization will be anxious to talk about your new focus on what membership dues are purchasing.

Meet with any active volunteer groups. Involved advocates can serve as great opinion leaders with others for getting out the word that things are, indeed, changing and improving. These groups can play a meaningful role in influencing and shaping broader owner opinion and encouraging support. Consider establishing a Key Communicator Network of opinion leaders for ongoing communication. In Appendix E, we include an outline for starting such a network.

If yours is a public board, meet with various community organizations. You will know which ones exercise influence and sway opinion: business and civic associations, Rotary Club, Elks Club, Cattlemen's Association, Chamber of Commerce, League of Women Voters, etc. Schedule a session for a board member to provide an overview of your new venture and its dominant focus on Results.

Conduct surveys. Lay the groundwork for change by conducting surveys, via the web, paper, or telephone, on what your owners expect. By asking their opinion, people become part of the solution and will be waiting for further information and perhaps involvement.

Some boards hire public relations specialists to assist them in developing a plan for communicating with various stakeholder groups. Some organizations have communications experts on staff assigned the duty of supporting the board in its communication efforts. Other boards form a "Communications/ Engagement Committee" to formulate a plan to recommend to the board. We have no specific preference about the source of support, but for all organizations, especially larger or more complex organizations, the board will need support from some such source.

As we have said before, there is no one way to do this work—just do it! Resources are available to help you define what works best for you, initially and over time.

FUNDAMENTAL TWO-WAY ENGAGEMENT CONCEPTS

Establishing a conversation of give-and-take is the beginning of a meaningful relationship between the board and its owners. This is always best done face-to-face, where the board can watch faces and body language, ask follow-up and probing questions, and allow members of diverse groups to hear feedback that may be diametrically opposite to their own opinion. They hear and hopefully appreciate the challenge posed by this diversity of views as you perform your governing role.

FOCUS GROUPS

We recommend focus groups as one strategy for engaging your owners and stakeholders in order to achieve the outcomes that we discussed above. The primary purpose of engaging in a focus group dialogue discussion is to share information about board work and to gather information from the group about issues of concern to the board. The focus group format, which features a hand-selected group of ten to twelve individuals representing an identified segment of your ownership, is good for depth of discussion about a few topics. It is not as useful if the board is interested in a broader sounding of opinions about many topics. See Appendix F for an example of conducting focus groups focused on one topic.

The focus group is not intended to provide an opportunity for the group to unload its issues on the board. There are ample opportunities for that to be accomplished without allowing a very positive, informative conversation to degenerate into a gripe session.

- *The board should determine the major components for the focus group session,* including:
    1. identification of the topic;
    2. identification of, and invitation to, participants;
    3. location and timing;
    4. the questions to be asked;
    5. welcoming, conducting, and ending the meeting;
    6. ensuring that all appropriate physical arrangements are made; and
    7. ensuring that participants receive appropriate follow-up.

- *Topics for focus group conversations, at least initially, primarily should be about the board's Results policies.* In our experience, many participants will want to steer the discussion toward operations, and, in fact, there may be instances when the board will want to discuss some operational concern. But Results should be the centerpiece of the board's work, and therefore should be the normal topic of focus group discussions.
- In determining individuals or groups for invitations, *the board should decide whose opinions would be informative to the board.* The people who are invited should receive personal written invitations *from the board* (not staff; this is board work) with a response card attached.

    Some boards attach a list of all people who have been invited in order to show each invitee that he or she is among a select group and will be missed if s/he fails to accept. Appropriate follow-up to the invitation via telephone also may be necessary.
- *Limit the number of questions to four or five.* This number of questions should allow for reasonable give-and-take and for follow-up, probing questions to be asked. We cannot overstate the importance of carefully constructed questions. Good questions lead to good answers.
- If the board decides to hold focus group conversations with several small groups on the same topic, *ask the same questions of each group.* This allows the board to compare what it has heard from each group and to see similarities as well as differences.
- *After each session, quickly debrief what you have heard and share salient points with the whole board.* After having heard from a number of groups, the board should schedule a debriefing session to allow it to get a broader picture, an overview, and decide whether further action or policy work is needed.

- *Settle on a schedule that adds minimal additional work for members.* If engagement meetings can be appended to the regular board meeting or to some other event, days and evenings can be saved.
- *Each focus group meeting should be around ninety minutes in length.* It is difficult to get much done in less than ninety minutes, and people are less productive if the meeting lasts longer than that. Start and end on time!

BEYOND FOCUS GROUPS

In considering engagement strategies, the board should decide whether it wants and needs small, informal give-and-take discussions with relatively small homogeneous groups (clergy, business interests, students, seniors, parents, etc.), or whether it wants to hear from larger, more diverse groups. This decision will depend on many factors, including the need to get broad input fast from many people, as opposed to gathering more in-depth information from identifiable groups over a longer period of time.

As a rule, the full board participates in all engagement discussions, if possible. In some organizations, it may be necessary, at least in part, to divide the load to get the job done. However, when less than the full board hears what is being said, something is lost when the discussion is translated to the whole board.

Some boards choose to divide into groups to conduct engagement discussions because of the size and complexity of the organization or community of owners the board serves. In such cases, we always recommend that at least two members participate in each meeting. This offers the advantage of at least two perspectives about what was heard, as well as lessening the load for any one member.

Of course, the strategies for meaningful engagement are limitless. Factors to guide choices are, of course, time, money, and expertise. Appendix G includes multiple strategies in a broad engagement plan. In addition to focus group-type discussions with small groups, boards very effectively have used such strategies as:

- *"Town hall" type meetings*, in which everyone with a stake in the organization is invited. These need to be carefully organized and facilitated in order to help the group stay on topic and to ensure that people feel heard and not just preached to about a topic. People tend to participate in such meetings only when the topic is one in which they are passionately interested. Otherwise, it is easy for them to skip another meeting. Proper room setup is critical. "Rules of engagement" must be carefully stated at

the beginning. The board must ensure skilled facilitation, and the meeting should conclude with a statement about the next steps the board will take with what it has heard.
- *Surveys* can be effective tools to use to collect information and inform the board's next steps. Either paper or electronic surveys might be considered. Paper surveys can be expensive if done comprehensively. Digital surveys (Survey Monkey, Mail Chimp, etc.) can be much less expensive, and can be done in a series of steps driven by specific topics that build on each other. Remember, the formulation of the questions is critical.
- *"Public engagement"* sessions facilitated by neutral parties. This allows the board to listen and learn without the pressure of conducting the meeting.
- *Study circles* is an innovative approach for problem-solving specific issues (www.studycircles.org).
- *"Key Communicator"* involves discussions with a preidentified group of opinion leaders. This process requires some up-front work to identify people who are well-regarded for their interest in your organization and its role within your community or membership. Meeting with the same people on a regular basis eliminates the time-consuming work of trying to set up and meet with many varied groups. Key Communicators can provide wise counsel to help the board navigate challenges, and at the same time enable the members to learn about the board's challenges firsthand so they become supporters and advocates for your mission.
- *Expert forums* allow for the arrangement of discussion sessions featuring noted experts on specific topics of critical interest to your owners. The board becomes the "thought leader" to highlight issues for broader understanding and to build support. Examples might include:

Education: Business icons discussing the skills and knowledge their businesses need from today's graduates to be successful employees.
Mental Health: Professionals discuss the impact of reductions in government funding to mental health programs.
Law enforcement: Judges discuss trends in the judicial system, or law enforcement officials discuss crime trends and statistics.
Senior Care: Professionals share about trends in serving this element of our population in ways that keep families together—at home.

The task is to identify strategies that make sense to the board, given the nature and complexity of the organization and its ownership, and the issues that need to be addressed.

As we have already mentioned, regardless of the strategies the board selects, it will need adequate support to make the engagement function successful. This support may not necessarily require added staff, but from some source—existing staff, volunteer help, board committees, or a combination of all—some detailed planning and logistical support work must be performed. Putting that element in place early will serve the board well when the engagement work begins.

A TEMPLATE: HOW TO GET STARTED

The strategic and organized full board focus on continuing interaction with the owners and stakeholders very likely is work the board has never done before. So, just how does a board, especially one with limited support resources, shift its attention to the task and start performing the role with some degree of proficiency?

Exhibit 7.1 is a "fill in the blank" template for creating a communication plan for the board's engagement with its owners and stakeholders. The full board makes the final decision about all the components, including meeting format, dates, people to be involved, the questions to be asked, and other related details.

School Board Engagement Plan

Exhibit 7.2 is a template that was created to help a large school board client establish an initial communication plan to engage its owners.

Survey to Complement Personal Engagement

As we discussed earlier, surveys can contribute to the board's base of knowledge about the topics being discussed with groups during face-to-face sessions. The survey can be used to supplement the information gathered at engagement meetings, and even after board business meetings. Exhibit 7.1 is an example of a survey used for such purpose.

Exhibit 7.1. Stakeholder Engagement Plan

What?
Who?
Where?
When?
How?

What topic(s) do we want to discuss?	A.
	B.
	C.
With whom will we meet?	A.
	B.
	C.
	D.
Who meets with them?	A.
	B.
	C.
	D.
Where do we meet?	A.
	B.
	C.
When do we meet?	A.
	B.
What linkage strategy do we want to use?	
What questions will we ask?	1.
	2.
	3.
	4.

Exhibit 7.2. School Board Engagement Plan
Board committee makes initial plans to recommend to the Board.

What?

Who?

Where?

When?

How?

What topic(s) do we want to discuss?	A. Broad overview: Beliefs, Vision, Mission B. Major focus: Student achievement goals • Valuable enough to be actionable? • Perceptions? • Impact?
How and with whom do we meet? Index: D=district dialogue F=focus group K=key communicators C=community O=other S=survey L=liaison	• Existing advisory groups • Cultural groups (F) • Most recent graduating class (F) • Leadership Team (F) • Current students (F) • Faith-based community (K, F) • Civic/homeowner assns. (D, K) • Business community (F, K) • Community leaders (K) • Parents (D) • Senior citizens/retirees (F, K) • Principal assns. (S) • Teachers and employees (S) • Legislators (O)
Who on Board meets with them?	• Focus Groups: significant number of members (4–6) • District Dialogue: host district member plus at least one other member • Key Communicators: entire BOE • Expert Community Forum: entire BOE • Other: entire BOE • Advisory Board Liaisons: appointed member plus one
Where do we meet?	A. Board and Director of Communications will devise method/process for logistics B. The Board will meet where it is most convenient for the invitees
How do we meet? Linkage strategies to consider, both short and long-term.	*Focus Groups* (12–15 people representing defined group) *District Dialogues* (come one-come all meeting in member districts; involves at least host-member and one or more other members) *Key Communicators* (continuing group of 40–50 key opinion leaders from throughout county; meet quarterly for two-way conversation with entire board *Community Forum* (come one-come all meeting; initial full-group presentation, then facilitated sub-groups with all members facilitating) *Longer term strategy*

(continued)

Exhibit 7.2. *(Continued)*

When do we meet?	• Weekdays • District dialogue – evenings • Focus Groups – dependent on group • Keep under 2 hours (7-9 or 6-8 PM) • Key Communicators: bkfst or lunch
What questions do we ask?	1. What expectations do you have of a graduate of our school system? In other words, what should they be prepared to do? 2. Do you believe these goals will accomplish those expectations? 　• Are they appropriate and relevant? 　• Are they ambitious enough? 　• Are they too ambitious? 3. How will we be able to determine whether students achieve their potential? 4. The Board has identified what it considers to be essential life skills. Are there other specific skills you would add to this goal? 5. How would students demonstrate that they are productive citizens?
During and After Linkage Sessions: Synthesizing Process	• Provide a recorder for each meeting. • Record either on flip chart or laptop/overhead (or both) • Use a consistent format for presentation of meeting outcomes (Q&A) • Board member debrief with each other directly after each meeting; information will be captured electronically by staff and then be shared with the rest of the Board members in an executive summary format consistently throughout the entire process 　◦ Summary response to each question 　◦ Debriefing summary 　◦ Individual Notes • Staff members will synthesize responses as the process continues, noting trends and themes
Next Steps	• Craft an invitation that attracts attendees. Must be compelling. • Develop exit survey. • Identify and invite individuals to key focus groups. • Notify community about meetings using district channel, school newsletters, local media. • Meeting participants sign-in sheets with email address for follow up. • Follow up: "Thanks for coming; here's what we heard; here's what we're going to do with the information." • Notify all participants when the synthesized goals are completed. • Publish final product for the world, needs to be translated. (same outlets as above)

EXHIBIT 7.3. COMMUNITY ENGAGEMENT SURVEY

We feel a vital need to work with our citizens and parents to focus on and increase the level of achievement with *all* of our students in this district. Would you take a few moments and respond to the questions we are asking below? We are attaching a copy of our Student Achievement Goals for your reference.

We will share the summarized survey responses with you at our fall community forum. We will also share with you our responses and plan of action at that time!

1. The goals are in the School Board's priority order; do you agree with that priority?

    Yes __
    No __
    If not, how would you prioritize them?

2. You have $10 total to spend; how would you allocate it among the three?

    Academic Achievement: $ __
    Life Skills: $ __
    Citizenship: $ __

3. What barriers exist to prevent our children from achieving these goals?

    a.
    b.
    c.

4. Will you attend the follow-up meeting in the fall to hear the results of all citizen feedback and board focus on student achievement goals?

    Yes __
    No __

5. What do you believe are the greatest issues challenging our district in working to improve achievement?

    a.
    b.
    c.

(continued)

> **EXHIBIT 7.3.** *(Continued)*
>
> 6. What recommendations can you offer to increase our effectiveness as a whole board as we work to focus on meeting the diverse needs of *all* students?
>
>   a.
>   b.
>   c.
>
> 7. From where do you receive your most reliable information about the board and its work?
>
> 8. How would you prefer to receive information from your board member and the board? (Please circle your highest preference.)
>
>   newsletter
>   web site
>   email
>   regular meetings
>   television
>   other (please identify):
>
> 9. What kind of information do you most want to hear about from your board member and board?
>
>   Thank you for your time and interest!

KEY COMMUNICATORS: STRATEGIC COMMUNICATIONS

We wrote earlier in this chapter about Key Communicators as one engagement strategy. A Key Communicator group simply is a selected group of "key" people in the community of owners, or individuals who have demonstrated interest in the organization and its welfare. They are people who tend to have credibility with the broader community, people who command respect and attention when they speak or offer an opinion.

Key Communicator groups tend to be comprised of visible people in the community or organization, including some people who may hold an important position. However, others well may be individuals in the community who may not carry impressive titles, but nevertheless are opinion leaders among those with whom they interact.

Consider these possibilities: a former board member, a popular breakfast café manager, stylists at the local salon or the barber, an activist parent, a former association president. In selecting people to serve, the board should look beyond titles and position, and determine the most listened-to people among various elements of the broader ownership.

To create such a group, the board identifies up to thirty or so people it considers to fit the qualification profile. Then the board invites them to meet for insider organizational updates and to learn and to share information, both ways.

Since Key Communicators requires members to serve on an ongoing basis rather than committing to just a onetime interaction with the board, the board will need to build into the process a bit more formality. This helps to ensure that the group performs a contributing service and does not become, over time, a controlling body rather than a contributing one. We recommend that the board invite participants for a one-year term only. Some members could be asked to return for another year, if the board chooses, but we encourage the board to guard against creating lifetime appointments for this or any other group.

Appendix E includes a suggested process to activate a Key Communicator group as an ongoing communication strategy.

HOW ONE SCHOOL BOARD ENGAGED THE COMMUNITY TO DISCUSS RESULTS ON CITIZENSHIP

What a timely and hugely important Result in our complex world: citizenship. It is a potentially divisive topic for a community to discuss. One proactive school board conducted a series of dialogue sessions, which the board called *"Voices to Vision."* The board held meetings across its very large and diverse community, focusing on the board's newly developed Results policies.

The purpose of the engagement campaign was to gather input from community members/owners about the importance of student citizenship and participants' willingness to help students become model citizens. The process yielded remarkably consistent Results among respondents, both within each meeting and across the community.

Appendix F includes the abbreviated documents associated with this campaign, including the original Citizenship Result, the focus group agenda, and meeting protocols.

HOW ONE SCHOOL BOARD PROACTIVELY RESPONDED TO CHALLENGE

A school board was challenged with significant internal divisions, some very trying district-wide circumstances, as well as state-level political dynamics.

The board determined the need to quickly engage with its owners about its new focus on Results and increased accountability of the superintendent.

In order to sustain members' focus and lead the community to support the board and district efforts, the board, with the aid of its director of communications, developed a comprehensive and strategic communication plan for the board's short-term use in dealing with the issue. The final detailed example is included in Appendix C. Note that the *Board Listening Campaign* focuses on the informal Key Communicators strategy.

THOUGHT LEADERSHIP: HOSTING A FORUM FEATURING EXPERTS

An important part of the board's job description is to provide leadership. That sometimes means opening doors of thought that people may not have realized needed to be opened. It can mean taking people—the board's owners, primarily—to places they otherwise might never go. It can mean getting ahead of the curve, generating an understanding of new realities that will impact your organization. It can mean leading the thoughts of people.

One way the board can accomplish this purpose is to arrange for meetings and host outside experts who know and understand those realities. At least two boards we have worked with have done just that, as illustrated in Exhibit 7.4. These forums are opportunities to "lead" the owners to a focus on the organization's future, and to build support for creating a new future for the organization without waiting for others to impose that focus. The board is seen as the thinkers, the leaders, rather than as passive reactors to the agendas of others.

If such a strategy is chosen, the board should consider:

- Go after *big guns!* Many very well-known and well-respected individuals are very accommodating to this kind of work (watch *YouTube* and observe Bill Gates and Warren Buffett in a forum with college students, hosted by the college board of trustees).
- Keep the panel to no more than two people.
- Keep it casual, but fast-paced and provocative.
- This strategy is not unlike hearing a thought-provoking speaker(s) at a convention. The difference here is the board is the host and convener, and should be recognized for the effort to stimulate new thought with a purpose in mind.

EXHIBIT 7.4.
THOUGHT LEADER COMMUNITY FORUMS

Venue: Two community-wide forums: one evening/following morning
Date:
Objective: Provide initial broad-based awareness of the board's work in focusing on skills and character for world-class students.

- Three-hour seminar: Hosted by "your board"
- Topic: Future skills and character discussion by two experts (possibilities: a futurist, Thomas Friedman, David Brooks, Warren Buffett, Bill Gates, Elon Musk, Madeleine Albright, Condoleezza Rice)
- Promotions: Web, TV, letters from schools, ad in the local papers and community weeklies. Taped and replayed on the school channel.

Agenda

Minutes
:15 Opening remarks and welcome: board president
:60 Panel presentation
:60 Questions from the audience of citizens and students for interaction
:20 Governing Board questions/comments to the experts; preidentified and fast-paced
:10 Wrap-up: Speakers
:05 Adjourn: President

Invitation/message

The ___ School Board invites you to join them
in a forum with leading national experts
Critical Learning at a Critical Time . . . for World Class Students

How Do We Prepare Our Students for *Their* Tomorrow?
- Language: Do they need to know two? More?
- Skills: Collaborate? Principle-based decision-making?
- Role of values, religion, working with those "different" from themselves
- How does a world-class system REALLY deliver world-class instruction for world-class learning?

STAKEHOLDER ENGAGEMENT: IN SUMMARY

For some reason, creating and executing an engagement plan for boards causes consternation and often results in prolonged delays. Some boards get overwhelmed when they consider all the questions associated with the challenge:

- Where do we begin?
- How can we get already busy board members to commit more time?
- How do we accommodate members who are shy of public speaking?
- Will the organization's staff be supportive, or will they feel imposed upon if they are asked to support the board's engagement plans?
- Can the board sustain *its* plan and not allow it to spin off into a staff-driven venture?

All are good questions and legitimate concerns. But boards can and must engage with the people they are committed to lead, serve, and represent if their role is to be performed effectively. How can any board effectively execute its job of leading and representing its owners if it doesn't understand those owners' expectations and if it does not have those owners' support? These are the dual purposes of a well-designed engagement plan, and they can be met only if the board takes this element of its job description seriously.

It is apparent that developing an effective engagement plan for the governing board of a large and complex organization is a significant task for a part-time board of directors to undertake. If the organization is relatively small and "compact," the task may be much easier. But for the board of a larger organization with a broad ownership base, support and guidance from someone who understands the intricacies of effective communication will be invaluable.

This is hard work, but it can be some of the most important and rewarding work the board will do.

QUESTIONS FOR THOUGHT

1. Does your board now have a plan to communicate with its owners?
2. When and how do you—as a full board—deliberately engage with the people the board serves and represents?
3. What is the difference between individual members' interacting with people within their own circles and the full board's role in owner interface?

FAQS

Q: How do we get started? Is it one board member or a committee or a staff member who leads the effort?

A: Logic and experience prevail here. Usually one board member will volunteer to draft a plan and bring it to the full board. Sometimes it falls to a committee of the board to draft the plan, or to identify a staff or community communication expert to work with two or three members to do the draft plan. It is not advisable to delegate the development of the board's communication plan to the staff, since this is a board function and requires the board's hands-on involvement. Don't default to staff to "lead"; this is board work. Own it!

Q: How can we gain full board commitment to spend the time and effort to make this work?

A: First, majority rules. Vote and move forward. Then make the efforts so interesting, the topics so critical, that no one wants to be left out. Get the train out of the station and they will jump on board.

Q: Beyond time, this sounds like money.

A: Yes, it will require some resources. Remember in your GC-2.4, Governing Commitments, the board expressed its value that it will assure budget support necessary to do its job. Be prudent—but find the resources and allocate them to engage with your owners.

Q: What role does the CEO play in meetings?

A: Minimal. This is board work, and attendees should focus with you on board work and governance priorities. It is appropriate for the CEO to attend all such events, but if the CEO takes the lead, almost inevitably the focus turns to operations. Keep this effort focused on the board and its defined Results and challenges that require board support and advocacy—and the understanding of the people you serve.

Chapter Eight

The Board's Annual Work Plan

Most boards have no idea what they will be working on from one meeting to the next. They have no defined schedule for their work, and consequently they tend to spend most of their time doing whatever someone else says they should do, or whatever feels right at the time.

An annual work plan is a built-in feature of your Coherent Governance or Policy Governance method of doing business. We have never worked with a board that, once acquainted with the idea of using a work plan for a full year, ever abandoned that excellent tool for good governance.

Planning its own annual work empowers the board to exercise leadership for the organization, to regulate its workflow, and to demonstrate its accountability to the owners—all based on a logical, thoughtful sequence.

All organizations and work teams perform better when they plan their work. The purpose of planning is to help the board move logically into the future, doing the things that the board thoughtfully has identified as its priority work. This deliberate and careful planning prevents the board from reacting to the crises of the day, or equally misguided, spending time doing whatever the agenda has on it, regardless of the board's view of what is important.

The annual work plan is also the basis for establishing each board meeting agenda, which should be developed by the board president in conjunction with the CEO. The board's scheduled actions and discussions are transferred at the designated time from the work plan to the regular board meeting agenda, and therefore define the board's ongoing work. The work plan allows the board to schedule its work in these important areas:

- GC monitoring
- BCR monitoring
- OE monitoring

- Results monitoring and related work
- Engagement with owners and stakeholders
- Board development
- Any other tasks or events the board should plan its work around

The annual work plan offers the board an opportunity to assume responsibility for its own work and to anticipate thoughtfully the issues its meeting agendas should include. These are some of the questions that drive the scheduling of the work plan as the last step before adoption of the policies and venturing into this new world of governing:

1. When should the board self-assess? Does it want to do all GC and BCR policy monitoring at one time during an annual retreat? Should the board divide the work into quarterly sessions? Would self-monitoring be done better in work sessions? Should a third party be engaged to facilitate monitoring?
2. When should OE reports logically be presented in coordination with other functions of the organization, such as the financial audit?
3. When will data be available during the year that may drive the scheduling of Results monitoring reports? How can the board logically receive interpretations and indicators prior to monitoring progress? How much time will it take? Does it require full meeting, or more than a single meeting? Which activities should be scheduled within a regular meeting? Does the board need a special meeting? Should the board schedule its first consideration of monitoring reports at a work session as a means for more thorough and informal give-and-take?
4. Which owner engagement sessions does the board want to schedule, with whom? Will these be separate meetings, or coordinated with the board's regular meeting schedule?
5. What other commitments does the board have—conferences, conventions, audits, etc?

The CEO and staff are well-served by having ample lead time—sometimes a full year—to prepare for the dialogue, deliberations, reports, and presentations the board has identified as important. Therefore, it becomes apparent that the annual board work plan is a tool not only to assist the board in scheduling its work, but also to help the staff organize its work in support of the board.

The annual work plan is not intended to be unchangeable; it can and should be modified as circumstances and events require—but only by the board. It is the property of the board, not of the CEO. If the CEO determines that some schedule change needs to occur, that change should be presented to the board for its concurrence. It is not within the CEO's purview to pick and choose which scheduled items to deal with or delay.

Even with the best of planning, things will change. For example, if a monitoring report is not fully accepted by the board (if one section is found to be noncompliant, for example), the board will want to add remonitoring of that one "exception" to the annual work plan. This prevents any necessary follow-up work from falling through the cracks. And both the board and staff know very well the expected timelines that must be met.

Although normally every Operational Expectation and every Result policy should be scheduled for monitoring each year, it may take a year or more for the board and staff to phase in full monitoring of all such policies. The organization is being asked to do work it has never done before, and in some instances, it will need time to develop new capacities to do that work well. The board and CEO jointly can decide just how much organizational stress is reasonable as early work plans are developed.

We are attaching samples of two annual work plans. Exhibit 8.1 represents a work plan for a board that meets monthly, as many public boards do. A monthly meeting schedule affords the board the opportunity to spread out its monitoring schedule and other work, as this work plan illustrates.

Exhibit 8.2 represents a typical work schedule for a board that meets quarterly. Note that all monitoring work is scheduled much more compactly, since the board has fewer opportunities during the year to schedule such work.

QUESTIONS FOR THOUGHT

1. What now drives decisions about the issues that make up your board meeting agendas? Are those decisions based on any pre-designed plan of work?
2. Do you have any idea about what your board will be working on at a given time during the next year?
3. How would scheduling the board's work for the next year change what your board spends its time doing?

Exhibit 8.1. Annual Work Plan

Month	GC	BCR	OE	Results	Dialog	Board Development	Other Business
Jan			6 M (EX) 13 RI			MBTI Training	
Feb			4 RI		Legislators	Negotiation Training	Retreat: CEO Formative Evaluation
Mar			2 RI/M 8 RI	2 ELA: RI		Parliamentary Procedure	Adopt governing policies
Apr			3 RI				
May			10 RI	2 Math: RI		NSBA	
June			11 RI	2 Science: RI			
July			1 RI	2 Soc St: RI		Wisdom Sharing	Teacher Negotiations
Aug	1–9	1–5	5 RI	1: RI		Retreat: Data Training Bd Self-assess	Retreat: CEO Summative Evaluation
Sept			6 RI/M (IN)	2: RI		State Assn. Convention	Craft SBA resolutions
Oct			9 RI	3: RI		Bargaining Training	Craft Legis Agenda
Nov			12 RI	4: RI		Listening Skills	
Dec			7 RI/M		Legislators		

RI = reasonable interpretation + indicators
BN = benchmark, comparative districts
M = monitoring for OE compliance or R reasonable progress
IN = internal monitoring
EX = external monitoring
B = baseline, year one
T = target

Exhibit 8.2. Annual Work Plan, Quarterly Meeting Schedule

Month	GC	BCR	OE	Results	Board Development	Engagement	Other Business
July			3 (RI) 4 (RI) 11(RI)	R-2 (RI) R-3 (RI)	Parliamentary procedure	Past clients	Audit
Oct	1–10	1–5	6 (RI) 9 (RI) 5 (M)	R-4 (RI) R-7 (RI)	Myers Briggs Type Inventory	Small company members	Board: Retreat Self-assess CEO Eval
Jan			2 (RI) 7 (RI) 1 (RI)	R-5 (RI) R-1 (RI)	Facilitation skills	Large company members	Annual Report
April			12(RI) 10(RI) 13(RI) 8(RI)	R-6 (RI)	Understanding data	Minority stakeholders	Board nominations

RI = Reasonable Interpretations & Indicators
M = Monitoring

AGI Aspen Group International, LLC ®

FAQS

Q: How flexible is the annual work plan?

A: By its very nature, the board's annual work plan may change at every meeting. It is intended to be a tool for scheduling the board's work. Depending on how monitoring reports are judged, engagement sessions change or are scheduled, or other work demands appear, items will be added, deleted, and moved from one meeting to another. This is a dynamic tool.

Q: How do we change the annual work plan as situations arise?

A: The board controls its own work plan. A majority vote is required to change the work plan. Staff can propose a change, but only the board can make it happen.

Q: Who maintains the calendar?

A: An administrative assistant to the board is the best choice. S/he should clarify any changes at board meetings at the time they are made. Meeting minutes should be accompanied by the updated work plan and sent digitally to members and senior staff.

Chapter Nine

The Board's New Meeting Agenda

Find a copy of your last board meeting agenda. Look at it closely. Now, take it outside, behind the barn. Dig a hole. Place the agenda inside. Now cover it. If you really mean what you say about your commitment to Coherent Governance, you'll never see anything like that again!

Based on our years of experience working with boards, we have discovered something remarkable: For the most part, boards will spend their time during meetings doing almost anything the agenda asks them to do. Something more: With few exceptions, those agendas are prepared for the board by someone else, usually by the CEO.

This means that meeting after meeting, year after year, a typical board will come to meetings, and spend sometimes hours and days, simply responding to the recommendations offered by the CEO about matters the board may or may not agree should be the primary reasons to meet. Or, maybe even worse, these boards may be held captive to a series of extended staff reports about who-knows-what, whether the board has agreed that it needs to spend its time listening to such reports or not.

Tradition often drives these repetitive and endless reports, and the board is reluctant to stop receiving them for fear of offending. Staff may dread developing them, but yet look forward to their hour on center stage in front of the board. It is rumored that a few CEOs schedule reports to "keep the board busy" and out of issues they would prefer not to have the board involved in. After all, boards will spend their time doing something, they reason, so why not keep members busy doing "stuff"?

This does not mean that CEOs are bad people, or even that they prepare illogical or self-serving agendas—although we all know that to be the case upon occasion. But what it does mean is that someone other than the board is determining what the board should do and when it should do it.

We are zealots about boards' developing and using well-constructed board meeting agendas. In fact, our conviction is that the board meeting agenda can be one of the single most important components for building an effective board. If the agenda asks the board to do the wrong work, boards usually will do the wrong work. Boards rarely reject an item placed on the agenda for them to deal with, whether it is legitimate board work or not.

How should your agendas—and therefore your board meetings—change in a Coherent Governance environment?

Let's review the basics. You said you wanted to:

- Move to Coherent Governance so your board could spend time doing important leadership and governance work;
- Spend far more time on the important Results the organization is expected to achieve;
- Stop micromanaging professional staff;
- Engage both proactively and constructively with those people you serve and represent;
- Free yourself from the drudgery, the mundane "fixing things" routine you had fallen into; and
- Take responsibility for your own agenda—driven by your annual work plan.

Does it make sense, then, that if all these benefits are to be realized, your meetings must look dramatically different? There should be no mystery here.

The board simply needs to ask itself, "What is it that we need to spend our time doing?" What are the issues that deserve the brainpower of five (or seven or nine or eleven or more) board members entrusted to lead, represent, and serve the owners' interest?

If the board agrees with the bulleted points above, then it must decide what should go away and what should be added to the agenda to realize these outcomes. Typically, these are the things board meetings will focus on:

- Discussing the future: Far-ranging and future-focused questions to ask include:
  ◦ What kind of benefits do our customers or members need that we can uniquely or competitively provide?
  ◦ What emerging trends are changing our lives and livelihoods that cannot be ignored and must be prepared for? Who can help us identify these trends?
  ◦ What is the gap between what students or members are accomplishing now and what they need to be accomplishing? What will our kids need

to know to compete and succeed ten years from now? How do we prepare them for multiple careers?
  - Are our present Results policies adequate to prepare our members or clients for such a successful future? If not, how should we change them?

- Monitoring your progress: With movement into implementation of Coherent Governance, relatively little business meeting time should be spent monitoring performance in the GC, BCR, and OE sections. More time will be spent monitoring progress in the Results policy areas. Questions to ask include:
  - Are the identified Results the "right" ones for our organization?
  - Are our resource allocations reasonable?
  - What are the barriers or hindrances to our progress?
  - Are there other factors or influences, internal or external, that we didn't anticipate?
  - Are subgroups of clients not adequately being served? Why? Are we willing to tackle this thorny issue, or do we ignore it because it is difficult to address?
  - How can we engage outside resources to improve?

- Stakeholder engagement: Questions to ask include:
  - Are our Results meeting community-of-owners' expectations?
  - Do our owners know how we are performing?
  - Are the owners or members prepared to discuss data revealing levels of acceptable performance and areas of underperformance?
  - With whom should we be establishing partnerships for the benefit of our clients and our owners?
  - Are there potential resources we should be taking better advantage of?
  - Who can help speed up our progress in a given Results area?

- Resource allocation. Questions to ask include:
  - Has anything changed that suggests another look at our initial resource allocation?
  - Are our plan and our priorities producing the desired Results?

- Priorities: We have acknowledged that we can't do everything in this area. Questions to ask include:
  - Are our priorities and our strategies aligned?
  - What will we not do—what do we need to let go of?
  - What is the fallout from not doing it?
  - With whom should we be communicating about these priority concerns?

Do you see a pattern in these questions? They are future-oriented, not reactive in nature. And they all are concerns that a governing board must consciously and responsibly confront. They are "big picture," not "what color carpet shall we buy" issues.

Of course, if you serve on a public or government board, *some* time must be spent dealing with the mandated items imposed by the state or federal government: approve the budget, approve personnel, approve new required operational policies, and such matters. Note the verb used here: *approve*, not *dwell on*.

The board can and should deal with these purely operational issues via the consent agenda, within the context of your well-defined Operational Expectations policies. Devote as little board meeting time to them as possible. Your very first OE policy requires the CEO to act legally. If state or federal law requires some specific action, the CEO cannot ignore it, whether the board makes a decision about the matter or not.

You are freed from making and remaking operational decisions because your values-based governing policies have directed and controlled operational decision-making and established rigorous accountability through scheduled monitoring.

But let's make the *main point*: The decisions the board makes should be *policy-level* decisions, not operational-level decisions. The board's new governance policy manual will be a dynamic document. You will have it handy at every meeting, because if you become a board that governs by policy, you will find yourself referring to a policy every time you meet, for every item on your agenda, and every time you make a decision.

And imagine this: You may have meetings of the board during which *no* decisions are made other than to adopt the agenda and to adjourn. You may find yourself listening, planning, understanding, exploring options, or visioning the future, without the need to decide anything. If so, you have not neglected your work. You have redefined it. You may find yourself faced with an agenda containing two or three—or maybe even only one—very focused, very deliberative, discussion item(s).

Remember, the board is seeking depth and quality deliberation on substantive issues. You will find that you won't be measuring the board's performance on the basis of how many decisions are made during a given meeting, but on the quality of your deliberative discussion and preparation for decision-making.

SO, WHAT WILL YOUR NEW AGENDA LOOK LIKE?

We cannot decide for the board exactly what its new meeting agenda should look like, the things that should be removed and the things that should be added. But we can offer some basic guidance based on some of the fundamentals of the new governing model.

Specifically, the new agenda must be built in a manner consistent with the board's job description, which is defined in policy GC-3. This is why:

- Does it make sense that the board performs its job, for the most part, in the board meeting?
- And does it make sense that the board meeting agenda should be very closely aligned with the board's job description, virtually a mirror image?

If we can answer "yes" to these two questions, the task is half complete. We need now only to set the board's job description, GC-3, alongside the agenda and align the agenda with the policy.

Of course, it isn't quite that simple or easy. There are some things on the board's customary agenda that it will want to keep for ceremonial or customary reasons, and others that may need to stay for legal reasons. But none of these agenda items should be centerpiece items. They should be limited in number and diminished in prominence.

The board has committed in policy to spend most of its time and attention on its Results policies. In order to do so, other kinds of items must go away or be subordinated.

Every type of organization will have some agenda components that tend to be unique to organizations of that type, but as a rule, there are some common agenda components that will serve every organization, regardless of type, very well. Appendices H and I include sample agendas with specifics to consider.

- *Adopt the agenda as the first action item.* Adopting the agenda means that the board commits by majority vote that this is the board's work plan for this meeting. The reason: to keep the board focused on the issues the board itself has agreed to consider, and nothing more. The proposed agenda is not the board's agenda until the board adopts it. That is why adoption of the agenda should be the first action item on the agenda. If any member wishes to add or remove an item (even from the consent agenda), to rearrange the order, or make any other changes to the recommended agenda, the time and means to do so is *before the adoption of the agenda*, by the amendment process.
- *Reference each item on your agenda to an existing board policy.* If you can't find a logical fit, it may be an indication that the topic is not board work at all! This policy reference step creates context, and prevents random discussions that tend to lower the board's focus to operations. Assigning policy references to each agenda item helps the board build knowledge and understanding of its own policies, and therefore should be done by members of the board itself, not by staff.

- *Place Results discussions toward the beginning of your meeting.* Staff and any audience begin to see that you mean business—customer- or client-focused business. High-performing boards spend at least 50 percent of their meetings focused on Results. Of course, if operational areas are not working as they should, or if other factors force the board's attention to them as opposed to Results, the board is doing the work it should. But if all operations are working as expected, there is no reason to dwell on such matters. The opportunity is presented to do a level of board work that most boards never find the time and occasion to do. But for you, such work now is routine!
- *Outline rules for audience or public participation*—and stick to them. This is the board's meeting, not the public's meeting. Hearing from the organization's members or from the public is common courtesy, but this should not be allowed to dominate or redirect the board from its central purpose.
- *Identify items to be disposed of via the consent agenda.* For the most part, these are the routine matters delegated to the CEO about which the CEO is required to keep the board informed. In fact, we recommend two consent agendas: a "CEO Consent Agenda," comprised of nothing more than board action on matters that have been delegated to the CEO, but required by a state or federal law to be approved by the board; and a second "Board Consent Agenda," comprised of any matter the board chooses to place on it, any item the board does not wish to spend time discussing. These two consent agendas help keep the board and CEO issues separate, and together can save considerable board meeting time—time to spend on Results. The sample agendas in Appendices H and I include samples of what some boards and CEOs place on consent agendas.
- *Time each section of the agenda.* Try to hold staff and yourselves to those times, without becoming a slave to the time estimates. The purpose of timed agendas is to help the board and its president or chair monitor the progress of the meeting and at least make members aware when estimated times have been exceeded or when the discussion becomes prolonged. Board meeting efficiency is not meant to be the primary goal, but it is important, and timed agendas can be enormously helpful.
- *Determine what staff presentations should look and sound like.* Do you want executive summaries of reports? How far in advance? Do you like PowerPoint presentations? Would you prefer that reports not be read to you? Are all reports referenced to policy and your monitoring schedule? The board never should show up for a meeting and be held captive to a series of staff reports, with no context, generally about process or programs that the board has delegated.
- *Make the final item on each agenda a verbal debriefing of the board's performance during the just-concluded meeting.* This need not be an extended

conversation, nor need it be an unpleasant personalized encounter. The idea is to provide an opportunity for the board to assess what worked and what did not, so that success can be repeated and failure can be avoided in the future. Consider debriefing the way the military does . . . an "After Action Review" that strategically positions your board for continuous improvement. At the end of this chapter, we offer some possible strategies for use in effective debriefing.

Sometimes the agenda may not be 100 percent "pure" or perfect according to the principles the board agreed to in Coherent Governance. But you will see the trends: There will be fewer agenda items; the focus will be bigger picture in nature; the agenda will be future-oriented; and fewer decisions will need to be made, with those decisions being made at the policy level.

Appendices H and I include sample agendas very similar to those used by boards practicing Coherent Governance. They generally track the provisions of the board's job description, GC-3. Use them as a starting point for the redesign of your own new agenda.

DEBRIEFING FORMATS

As with everything else in this book, there is no one accepted way to get work done. But in a broad sense, debriefing each meeting holds every board member to a higher standard of continuous improvement. Here are three ways for a board to conduct a meaningful debriefing exercise before the meeting is finally adjourned:

Option A. Three simple questions, posed by the chair or by a rotating member:

1. What did the board do well in our meeting?
2. What did not work well for us?
3. What do we want to do to improve?

Option B. Quick Whip Technique—each member responding to two distinct questions:

1. What elements of this meeting worked especially well?
2. What would I recommend to improve our overall performance for future meetings?

Option C. One member takes the lead:

One board member assumes the responsibility for closely observing the meeting and offers feedback to the board based on those observations. Other members respond to the leader's assessment with comments of their own. The role is rotated among members for each meeting.

ANOTHER MEETING ASSESSMENT OPTION: EXTERNAL MONITORING COMMITTEE

The External Monitoring Committee is a board committee created for the purpose of monitoring board meetings and reporting its assessments and recommendations to the board. The committee is carefully chosen for balance and credibility, trained, provided with copies of appropriate policies to monitor, and provided with agendas ahead of time.

An External Monitoring Committee can be very helpful to the board, and it can be a valuable supplement to the board's self-assessment process. The following report was submitted to a board that chose to appoint such a committee. This External Monitoring Committee was comprised of a group of stakeholders appointed by the board to observe the board's business meetings and offer constructive feedback. Members of the committee were trained in relevant policies and processes.

COMMITTEE FEEDBACK TO THE BOARD

Date:
To: Board Chair and Liaison
Fr: External Monitoring Committee—First Tuesday Team
Re: Debriefing of November 6 Board Meeting

Attached below is our feedback on the November 6 Board Meeting.

Commendation:

1. Meeting was well-officiated, exuded confidence.
2. Items on agenda were contextualized to relevant policy.
3. It appeared that the Board came to the meeting prepared.
4. The CEO and CFO delivered an oral summary of OE reports and read the reasonable interpretation aloud so that members could hear and consider. The Board showed interest in their reports.

5. The Board was very respectful of one another and of anyone presenting. There were no side conversations, and there was respectful body language.
6. The Board chose to be transparent in sharing its decision about the CEO and CFO compensation with the public at this forum.
7. The Board chair did an excellent job of managing issues raised during the presentations.

Example: During the presentation of the Reasonable Interpretation of OE-7 and OE-1, there were a few questions asked. The Board chair noted the questions, sought clarification, asked for the questions to be held until both OE-7 and OE-1 were completed. He came back to address each issue and ensured that the person bringing up the issue was satisfied with the resolution.

To Consider:

1. Post the board agenda so that the audience understands when the Board is in executive session.
    Example: The meeting officially started at 4:00 and went into Executive Session. The Public Session was started again at about 5:15 or so. It appeared to some in the audience that the board was late.
2. There appeared to be confusion about how to amend the agenda. It seems as if there should be a consistent process in place on how to amend an agenda.
3. There was no Results focus at this meeting—nothing related to student achievement.
4. Display Results policies on the walls of the boardroom—reinforce purpose and focus of the board.
5. This meeting lasted just about an hour; while none of us complained, it did make us wonder about the need for a meeting twice a month. We recognize the consent agenda was very long (about 144 pages) and realize there is a need to make sure it is approved twice a month, but we didn't really see the need for a meeting.

QUESTIONS FOR THOUGHT

1. How are your meeting agendas currently developed? By whom? Against what standards?
2. Boards generally find a way to debrief the effectiveness of meetings, either formally or informally. How does your board or its members debrief now? Is it a productive process?
3. Are your meetings driven by staff needs or board priorities?

FAQS

Q: Who should be responsible for developing the agendas for each board meeting?

A: The board meeting agenda is driven by the annual work plan. The board president, and possibly one other member on a rotating basis, generally meets with the CEO to develop the draft agenda. But it isn't the board's agenda until the board votes to accept it—the first action at the meeting.

Q: Who determines the policy reference for each item on the agenda?

A: Our strongest recommendation is that the board president and one other member on a rotating basis assume that responsibility. The policy reference decision needs to be made thoughtfully, since policy references provide context for deliberation and decision-making. The rotating member also monitors the meeting and leads the debriefing.

Q: How do we demonstrate that our work is focused on Results, when the agenda may have pages of consent agenda items that visually clutter it and make it appear that our work is all about operations?

A: We recommend that Results focus be placed high on the agenda, and that all detailed items associated with the consent agenda be placed in an appendix to the agenda. The ideal is for the agenda to be shown on a single typed page, with all the detail listed elsewhere.

Q: We have groups that are accustomed to reporting to the board, which makes our meetings appear to be dog-and-pony shows, consuming huge amounts of board time. How do we control that issue?

A: Consider whether some of the reports can better be received at a work session or presented to the CEO instead of to the board. Consider imposing time limits on all reports, based on their purpose and importance. If the board does not value such reports, they should not be a part of the meeting. The politics of this issue may require some delicate handling.

Chapter Ten

Change: It's a Leadership Conundrum

Boards and organizations committed to leading and driving organizational change must overcome a number of reasonably predictable barriers in order to achieve success. It isn't easy to do. It is more difficult in some types of organizations than others.

Large public organizations, such as school districts and other governmental entities, may be some of the most challenging of all environments in which to lead change. It can be done, for sure, but boards serving such organizations must have skills and a level of determination that allow them to maintain focus and commitment in the face of resistance that organizations of other types rarely ever face.

Below is a discussion of some of the common barriers to sustainable organizational change and improvement. If such barriers exist, they force a board choice: either stay the course and move forward with resolve to achieve the vision the board has for the transformed organization, or allow the barriers to thwart that vision the board had when this journey started.

BARRIER ONE: LACK OF SELF-DISCIPLINE

Admirably, boards want to honor differences of perspective and opinion among their members. But when board members "play nice" and fail to confront misdirected or errant behaviors, they marginalize and jeopardize organizational change efforts.

Lack of board discipline manifests itself in many ways: the errant chair who chooses to exercise individual power over the CEO; the board that fails to create its own meeting agendas, reacting solely to CEO-driven matters; the board that refuses to monitor its policy on board discipline and avoids confronting a misbehaving member; the board that finds debriefing untimely and abandons this quality improvement necessity; the board that passively self-monitors board behavior policies because rigorously doing so might stir confrontation.

You developed policies to govern board and board member behavior built on a set of shared values, and you committed to monitor the board's performance against those standards. Failure to hold the board and each member accountable tells the CEO, staff, and owners that the board didn't really mean it. Allowing the board or its members to misstep, or to intentionally and willfully violate your commitments, means the whole system is up for grabs. Why should any stakeholder group take the board seriously if it doesn't faithfully monitor and adhere to its own governing commitments?

Failure of the board, CEO, or staff to behave in ways that are consistent with the expectations and values serves only to increase cynicism and resistance to any transformation to excellence.

You made these commitments. You thought they were important. It is essential that the board honor the commitments if this transformation is to be effective and powerful.

BARRIER TWO: NOT INVESTING IN BOARD DEVELOPMENT

Change for a board and organization takes time, and it occasionally requires money. Some change experts say sustainable change requires a minimum of five years of focus and practice. The board may be able to change its own culture fairly efficiently, but leading complete organizational change should be expected to take longer. The larger and the more complex the organization is, the more difficult it is to imbed this change throughout the fabric of the organization.

For the board itself, our nanosecond level of patience seduces boards into straying off course, with members chasing the next diversion that appears to require their immediate attention. Even more frequently, we witness boards that tire of the structure and discipline of their new governing model and drift off to the more comfortable role of making operational decisions, "managing the manager," enjoying the role of fixing problems, and engaging in discussions and making non-board decisions because they perceive them to be important to "the community."

Transformation of board work and organizational focus begins with a board's sincere commitment to diagnose, address, and continuously critique its own governing style and performance. This requires disciplined adherence to a calendar that schedules continuous meeting debriefing, time spent in deliberative conversation with one another on issues of importance, and at least semiannual retreats in order to reflect, assess, prioritize, and establish systemic direction.

Board development includes thorough training both for candidates and for new members. In many organizations, board veterans provide orientation for people vying for the board so they know what they may be signing up for. Once new members are chosen, the board then provides thorough training for new board members by reviewing each policy, incorporating relevant changes, and renewing the board's mission and Results. The training is arranged by the board itself, prudently using their consultant, and is not delegated to the administration or to associations. Members learn together, coming to understand as colleagues how the board operates as a unified body in this special environment.

Other professional development areas needed by boards become apparent as members work closely together, focused on client outcomes. Gaps in knowledge or skills become barriers to Results achievement, and boards on top of their game recognize such challenges and take action to ensure that members are armed with the knowledge and skills necessary to lead effectively—even if reasonable costs are associated with such training.

For example, the Fairfax County, Virginia, school board engaged experts to help members increase their knowledge about twenty-first-century skills, one of the board's Results policies. The Issaquah, Washington, school board used data experts to help build board member skills as they considered Results monitoring reports. The Columbus, Wisconsin, school board engaged experts to help board members understand how to conduct focus groups. The school boards in Palm Springs, California, and Steamboat Springs, Colorado, used the Myers-Briggs Type Indicator to help members better understand each other and to work with mutual appreciation for diverse styles and behaviors.

Although funding always is a challenge, the reality is that good governance is worth something. A board committed to govern as well as it expects its employees to perform their jobs will recognize the need to invest reasonably in its own capacity and skill-building. Usually the money spent on board development is a mere fraction of what is spent for staff professional development.

BARRIER THREE: NOT CREATING AN INTERNAL URGENCY FOR TRANSFORMATION

The world is changing for organizations of every type. The marketplace presents new competitive realities that include pass/fail judgments.

Some wise person has said that change occurs only when "the pain of change is less than the pain of remaining the same." The successful change-demanding board recognizes the growing dissent and dissatisfaction with what many consider to be the high expenditure of dollars for mediocre Results. In the corporate world, evolution is a market-driven reality.

Every organization includes people who think in entrenched mind-sets, such as:

- "We've always done it this way, and we're doing okay; why change?"
- "Why would our talented staff members need to change the way they do business? After all, they are the professionals; they know their jobs."
- "How can a part-time board intelligently suggest such radical change?"
- "Wounded pride, bruised egos, and professional indignation can result when the board requires such dramatic change. Let's not rock the boat."

Audacious goals cannot be achieved by any organization when pockets of resistance work against organizational purpose and are permitted to fester. Real board leadership first requires clear definition of organizational mission and Results, and then, board encouragement and support for CEO efforts to take staff where they have never gone before. Strong CEO leadership will require deliberate assessment of barriers to excellent organizational performance, and the courage to do things differently. And when some employees cannot buy in to the vision for change, sometimes-tough decisions must be made by the CEO and supported by the board.

> "If it ain't broke, don't fix it", . . . is the slogan of the complacent, the arrogant or the scared. It is an excuse for inaction. It's a mindset that assumes (or hopes) today's realities will continue tomorrow in a tidy, linear and predictable fashion. Pure fantasy" (Colin Powell).

It is a battle to capture hearts, minds, and wills. And it's an important battle.

BARRIER FOUR: FAILURE TO COMMUNICATE

The board and its CEO must communicate strongly and frequently that *good is not good enough*. Excellent organizations create and sustain an environment that demands continuous assessment and positive, constructive support for improvement.

The old communication paradigm was to send out a newsletter or a press release. Put new goals on the web site. Have a community meeting. Deliver a rally call at the staff development kickoff for the new year.

Good, but not good enough. The communication from the board and CEO about their singular focus on Results must be consistent and repetitive, from day to day and from hour to hour. Each business meeting, each speech to the Chamber of Commerce and the Lions Club or member subgroup, each reply to a disgruntled patron, and each and every discussion with the CEO and staff about organizational performance begins with a re-grounding in the board's focus on Results.

If the board expects change to be embraced by the owners, the board must communicate with them. The establishment of ongoing dialogue about the board's Results; the changes to anticipate; honestly asking for help in diagnosing problems and barriers; encouraging questions to promote understanding before excoriating attacks are launched by the misinformed; engaging in advocacy efforts at local, state, and federal levels: All of these are issues the board needs to discuss with its owners.

The successful board of trustees reaches out and works with the people it represents, serves, and leads. That work cannot be accomplished if the board relies solely on outgoing messages and interaction with self-selected people attending board meetings.

The staff and owners must hear and see a board's long-term commitment to Results. The board must use every vehicle to communicate its vision and focus. Many boards have their mission and Results prominently mounted on the walls of their boardrooms. Many boards have highly interactive web sites and planned social media networks easily accessible by the owners. But the really successful boards also undertake their own strategic and planned engagement opportunities to build understanding and support for the organizations they serve.

As we discussed in Chapter 7, a wide variety of interactive engagement strategies exist for boards to explore and use: public engagement; study circles; focus groups; electronic surveys. We strongly urge boards to consider the advisability of retaining outside professional assistance to develop a highly strategic communications plan to meet the board's specific needs.

The critical keys to generating understanding and support for board and organizational efforts include asking good questions, listening well, using the feedback, and circling back for more discussion.

BARRIER FIVE: FAILING TO BUILD THE CORE AND REMOVE BARRIERS

The board cannot undertake this transformation in isolation. The CEO will be central to internal support and external credibility. If the CEO is a barrier, a controller, a power- or prestige-monger, or one who cannot accept the increased accountability, the board must recognize the fact that its vision may not be achieved under those circumstances.

The CEO must lead internal organizational change. Doing so includes challenging traditional protocols, removing obstacles to change, confronting and redirecting time and people, redesigning professional development, aligning personnel evaluations to Operational Expectations and achievement of Results, and activating new levels of freedom and accountability. The CEO is the internal organizational torchbearer.

Board members must build unity at their level, but the CEO must go shoulder-to-shoulder with the board to advance the vision. But even the board and CEO cannot perform that role in isolation.

The transformation team must include senior staff, critical administrators, union leadership, even community business and civic leaders who will support and advocate for the change efforts on an intimate level.

We have seen organizations where the change leader role is delegated to a staff member: the board clerk, the director of strategic planning, the chief of staff. That strategy simply does not work.

This kind of revolutionary work requires the visibility, urgency, strength, and extraordinary commitment of the senior executive with strong support from the senior administrative team. Failure to form a team characterized by such dedication means that little, if any, real change will take place. The result is the *pretense of progress*.

One large urban school board and staff intimately involved the business community and union leadership as the board moved into Coherent Governance. Working together in concentrated retreat sessions and subsequent strategy committees, together they built a coalition focused on strengthening the district and bolstering student achievement, all driven by the board's Results policies.

In Seattle, Washington, the CEO of a nonprofit organization was rigorous in leading the organization's focus on accountability. He redrafted his weekly board updates to reference each item directly to the relevant OE and Results policies. His tenacity in taking the board at its word—its policies—and constantly, consistently using them led the board to a greater understanding of its own governing model.

In a large southern school district, the superintendent worked with community groups to build support for board governance and for system integrity. She and her senior staff realigned staff development and conducted twice-yearly teacher evaluations to support teacher efforts to increase student achievement in alignment with the board's Results policies. The team included every principal.

The lesson: Without top-to-bottom organizational alignment, support, and commitment, systemic change will not happen.

BARRIER SIX: FAILURE TO KEEP IT UNDERSTANDABLE

Sometimes boards get so focused on their new governance system and its unique nomenclature they forget that there is a community of people who want to hear about the board's vision and purpose, but in plain language. Governance preoccupation and lexicon can get in the way of stakeholder acceptance and understanding. It is not the governance process you want people to focus on, but rather your vision for and necessary steps to achieve excellent organizational performance.

Some people talk about the "7/11" test. Can you state your vision for owner and client benefits within five minutes and without the need for a dictionary? Can you remove any language barriers that could entice people to gravitate to the negative when hearing something new and different?

Focus on the commonsense presentation of your expectations and organizational outcomes. If you can't make your work understandable to the person who does not live in your world each day, there will be no listening, no support, and eventually, no change.

BARRIER SEVEN: FORGETTING TO ADDRESS THE LEGACY

If sustainable change is to be embedded into the fabric of the organization, the values, vision, and systems put in place by the board and its team must outlive the current players. This calls for conscious planning for the recruitment and training of new board members. It also demands great forethought and preparation for recruitment and hiring of new staff, beginning with the CEO.

If you serve on an elected governing board and a vacancy is imminent, it is totally reasonable to cultivate and seek out individuals to run for election. Find potential candidates with the demonstrated character and capacity to engage with the board and organization in a constructive manner.

The "Power of One" never ceases to amaze us. The ability of a single board member to undermine and sabotage—or to inspire and exert new levels of leadership—is unlimited. A single member can do amazing good within a group of five, seven, or nine, but a single member can be equally harmful to the effective performance of a board. Fate must not be left to chance. Effective board leadership includes building capacity for sustainability and long-term momentum.

Sustainability and legacy also are issues with the board's only employee— the CEO. With CEO retirement or job change, what kind of leader should fill that pivotal role? Failure to recruit a CEO who understands that his or her role is to make *the board's* vision succeed can spell disaster for your change effort. Where do you recruit? Does the search firm understand your vision and how you do business? What does advertising language sound like? What kind of critical questions must be asked during the interview to ensure support for and compatibility with the board's governance system?

The experience of one very sophisticated organization comes to mind, one that did not pay attention to the true character of its final candidate—beyond his pretense during the interview to understand and support the board's governance focus and structure. Within the first year, the board was struggling due to the CEO's complete disregard for the board's work and his unwillingness to support it. No board wants to conduct a CEO search twice in a year, so the board was challenged to find ways to compensate for the shortcoming. The board's governance focus and processes since have recovered, but not without considerable challenge and tough board direction.

BARRIER EIGHT: IGNORING SUCCESSES

Most professions do very poor jobs of recognizing and celebrating successes. And yet, we all know that encouragement increases performance.

Boards often focus excessively on what fails to work. Sometimes it pays to acknowledge what's *right*! It is all in the balance, but the scales too often are tipped toward the negative.

Boards should identify shorter-term targets that increase the likelihood that reasonable progress can be made, and then celebrate when it occurs. The journey to higher performance is hard work, and to some, foreign work. Accountability can be threatening. Plan for, encourage, support, and praise the short-term successes to sustain momentum. The next day with its new challenges will come with the dawn.

Our life's work is based on hoping, believing, and coaching boards and their CEOs to break down traditional barriers and beliefs and become laser-focused on organizational performance. Doing so represents formidable change for many organizations. But we also know and believe that this country, and, indeed, the world, is populated by people who want to make a sustainable and constructive difference in the lives of the organizations they lead and the people those organizations serve.

Recognizing and removing barriers, externally or internally imposed, will augment the chances for successful change and attainment of that audacious vision boards have for their organization's success.

Chapter Eleven

Now What?

Your board has made the conscious decision to transform the way it does business. Traditional board work wasn't working well. Staff-driven agendas, useless policy, individual or even party politics, endless and mind-numbing debate about minutiae, and, quite probably, less than excellent organizational Results permeated your board life.

You concluded that your board must learn to govern with excellence—doing *its* job and no one else's—in order to direct and align organizational performance to achieve Results.

Your board consciously committed to good governance and chose a state-of-the art governing system, either Coherent Governance or Policy Governance, as the vehicle to get you there. At this juncture, your policies are in place, and you have implementation systems and processes ready to launch. You are confident that all systems are go, and that you are poised for a new purpose and greater rigor as a governing board. There are no storm clouds on the horizon. Life is good.

But hold on just a second. Although all the stars seem to have lined up just right at the moment, some challenging things could happen. Your board needs to anticipate and be prepared to deal with possible hazards. It is called risk management.

We encourage you to recognize that there is at least a slight chance that not everyone is as enthusiastic about your choice of a governing system as you are. These people could come from anywhere, either inside or outside the organization. They could even come from within the board itself.

The message here is that successful implementation of your new governing model is not automatically assured. In our first book, *Good Governance Is a Choice*, we discussed in Chapter 12 some of the essential conditions that boards and organizations must have in order to successfully implement a new governing model. We won't repeat all those points here, but we will recap some of them, since this is such an important concern.

WHAT COULD CAUSE YOUR WORK TO FAIL?

We have seen the following conditions contribute to failure:

Lack of Commitment by the Board

Common logic suggests that if the board was not committed, it would not have made the decision to adopt a new governing model in the first place. Sometimes common logic defies logic. Some boards are intrigued with the idea of doing something new and different, of being seen as a trailblazer, but less than fully committed to actually doing the work to achieve success.

Adopting a completely new and different governing model requires vigilant attention to new processes that will feel awkward for a while. Time and a little patience are necessary for the new work to gain traction.

Resist the temptation to suspend dedicated implementation practice and do it the "old way, just this once." Commitment means consistently walking the talk about your values. Stakeholders are observing you in action to see if you mean what you said: that you would be a disciplined board, focused on the achievement of Results, not on operations.

Resist the temptation to return to the practice of passing "resolutions" and giving informal direction to the CEO. Your commitment is to govern by policy, not by resolutions or by informal directives.

Resist the temptation to allow staff to report on process, rather than on compliance or progress. Presenting process information is not monitoring progress or compliance. This is not about being nice. It is about effective governing. Commit to the highest standard of performance by expecting and accepting nothing less than monitoring reports that clearly and consistently provide the information and data the board needs to judge performance, not activity.

Failure to Recognize That the Model Is a Means, Not the End

Adopting a new governance operating system is an important step for any board. At the beginning, there are new processes and behaviors to learn. It takes careful attention by the members to learn how to use the new tools available to the board.

But some boards are so consumed with "getting it right" that they become slaves to the system—the mechanics of doing the work—rather than focusing on the outcomes the system was designed to produce. They focus on the process with rigorous devotion rather than using the model as a way to get board work done.

There is a high level of discipline required of a board in order to live with the commitments it has made in policy. Nevertheless, within a reasonable period of time, the board and staff should be comfortable with this operating system as their adopted platform and practice, using it to focus on achieving Results.

Failure to Recognize That a New Governing Model Will Not Automatically Solve All Old Problems

Occasionally we have been invited to work with a board that is so dysfunctional that anything that floats by appears to be a life preserver. Sometimes boards find themselves in such distress that they adopt the view that if they can just adopt Coherent Governance, all their internal problems will go away.

Typically, the problems they are dealing with are as much people problems as they are structural problems: lack of trust, poor communication, controlling agendas and egos, a history of divisive behaviors, or a group of people who just don't like each other and who like to fight.

It is true that adopting a sound operating system can provide the structure to help boards deal with the tough people problems. Governance Culture and Board/CEO Relationship policies are designed to do just that. But until the board addresses such dysfunctional conditions, no governing system in itself will make life good again for such boards.

The Blame Game

Resist the temptation to blame the model when the first challenge hits—as it surely will. Commitment means understanding that change is hard to accept and sometimes viewed with intense skepticism. Stay the course, and your values for governing excellence will become clear, accepted, and welcomed. As time progresses, your governance system will become the norm. You'll find yourselves the board to be emulated.

Accepting Poor Behaviors

Resist the temptation to tolerate poor board or board member behavior or discipline. The board is judged by the quality of its own actions. Accepting anything less than consistent compliance with the board's commitments diminishes the integrity and effectiveness of the whole board. Commitment to excellence requires honest self-reflection and the courage to confront any individual or board failure.

A Board's Unwillingness to Deal Effectively with Overt Outliers

Even a single outlier can distract the board. Attention must be paid to those members who may not be in sync with the board majority. They come in all forms, ranging from willing but not enthusiastic, to true skeptics, to declared opponents, to outright saboteurs.

Those who are willing to join the board majority and try to make it work, despite some reservations, usually come on board. Their views are important and must be heard. Over time, there is a good chance that the board's success will elevate their level of support.

It is the saboteurs who concern us. These are the members who not only oppose what the majority is doing, but also try to ensure that the whole venture fails. Their overt and covert behaviors can take several forms, but you know them by their actions.

A board cannot allow individual members to divert its attention or waste its time. Nor can it allow the destructive behavior of a single member, or a distinct minority, to determine the board's fate. We still govern in a democracy, by majority rule. A number of possible remedies are available to the board to help deal with destructive internal behaviors, and they must be used as the board continues to seek to build unity and focus.

Unwillingness to Change Old Behaviors

It should be clear that adopting a different way of doing business requires old habits and customs to change. Some examples of traditional board behaviors that some find difficult to abandon include: committees with no clear role definition or old committees that were created to focus on CEO issues; undue authority given to or assumed by the chair; board meeting agendas developed and presented with no board control; allowing items to be pulled habitually from the consent agenda by a single member; CEO issues presented for board approval; continuing board preoccupation with operational issues.

We are not saying that every past practice is unworthy, but rather suggesting that a board must be willing to free itself from past practice and create a culture that is based upon thoughtful exploration of what is possible when a board focuses on Results, not what is comfortable. It calls for historical perspective and appreciation, but not living in history.

Impatience

Changing to a new way of getting work done requires time and practice. When we work with boards, we frequently ask members to write their names on a piece of paper. Then we ask them to place the pen in their opposite hand, and do it again. Then we analyze what they experienced.

They typically say that the second time was slower, messier, awkward, and required more attention and thought. In general, the nonpreferred hand was less efficient, with a less-desirable, even childish outcome.

Implementing a new governing model can feel that way. In order to become a mature board, to gain efficiency and achieve the desired outcome, new behaviors must be learned and new skills developed. This requires time, studied practice, and patience.

Just as reading, playing golf, playing the piano, building a sports team, or becoming an excellent speaker requires time and repetition, so does the practice of good governance. This is why we strongly encourage boards to maintain an extended coaching relationship, providing an outside "eye" to identify performance issues and maintain momentum as the board transitions into the mature practice of its new governing model. Remember, even champions need coaching.

A CEO Who Lacks Confidence in His Own Abilities, Who Is Unwilling to Assume Accountability for Independent Actions, or Is Unsupportive of the Board's New Role

Some CEOs say they support the board's venture into a governing model that allows them to exercise independent leadership and to be held accountable for it. But they continue to seek board approvals for decisions that are now theirs to make—reacting either out of fear or tradition.

Some CEOs openly resist the board's new level of governing leadership and policy-level control, setting up roadblocks of infinite types. Some view this venture as a means to "control" the board, only to discover that the board actually becomes more active—but in a constructive and less-intrusive way.

Other CEOs may be unwilling to change their own administrative behaviors to align the organization with the board's governing culture. They may have become very accustomed to functioning as the "leader" of the board, controlling information and giving direction to achieve their own purpose and ends.

When a board adopts Coherent Governance or Policy Governance, it changes not only its own way of doing business, but maybe equally dramatically, it changes the way the organization does its work. If a CEO either is unwilling or incapable of transforming the organization as necessary to support the board, the board's good work can be painfully slow or jeopardized.

Both Coherent Governance and Policy Governance can create the most freeing environments imaginable for the skilled, confident CEO. But they can be oil on water for a CEO who lacks the confidence and competence to do the job free of board approvals or who is resistant to assuming accountability for Results and doing quality monitoring of the organization's performance.

Lack of Support Necessary for the Board to Succeed

Adopting a new governing model requires more support for board processes than the old system required. The board must have designated and very competent staff support to assure rigorous, accurate, and on-time monitoring records; to maintain the annual work plan; and to manage the logistics of a stakeholder engagement plan.

WHAT TO DO WHEN PROBLEMS HIT

Sooner or later, your governing model will become a target. Count on it. It will happen. The only things we don't know are where the challenge will come from, and when it will happen.

If you are a public board, such as a public school board, it likely will happen fairly soon. The environment in which you work is volatile and visible, as well as laden with a full range of emotions and differing opinions about every decision. That environment presents easy opportunities for people to challenge everything—your governing model included. Even if how you make decisions and how the organization is governed have nothing whatsoever to do with the matters that concern people, they likely will label your governing model as the cause of whatever the real issue is.

Once the organization experiences a problem or makes a decision with which some people disagree, the board should be prepared to deal with charges that it has "given away the store" to the CEO. The board has "abdicated its responsibilities," and no longer is in charge. "Why even have a board," people will ask, "if it refuses to make decisions?" (All about operational issues, of course.)

Such challenges and criticism could come from within the organization, from staff or their organizations. Or criticism may come from outside the organization, from organized groups or influential individuals. The more inflammatory the issue, the stronger the challenge to the governing model will be. The board will be tempted by these groups to "get itself back in charge" and "do its duty" by overturning the administrative decision that caused such uproar.

Occasionally, the problems may be real. For example, the CEO may make a decision that runs counter to the board's policy values, and the board is required to respond in some fashion. In the old way of doing business, the board likely would jump into the middle of the issue and "fix it."

But whether the criticism is based on a real problem or not, it still becomes a challenge to the board's governing system. And it presents to the board an opportunity to respond. How would a board response in this new governing environment be any different from the way it might have responded under its old way of doing business?

A board's best course of action in any such challenge is to use the tools its governing model provides. We frequently say to boards as they are first launching their practice of the model that what they have is a shiny new toolbox, just loaded with all kinds of neat tools. Simply owning the tools is of little value to the board, however. In order to gain any real benefit, the board must actually use the tools as they were intended to be used.

These tools—your policies and the proper use of the processes we discuss in this book—are the board's best means for dealing with challenges such as those mentioned above. People who fail to understand the power of this system that delegates decision-making—but holds the people who make decisions accountable—need educating. And the board should be skilled in using the tools to demonstrate accountability, whether decisions are controversial or not.

Effectively monitoring organizational performance is an ongoing role of the board. If stakeholders both inside and outside the organization see the board doing its job on a continuing basis, they will be less likely to challenge the system when a decision is made that they don't like.

The board has the opportunity to monitor any policy at any time there is a need to do so. When criticisms are leveled, sometimes the board's logical course of action may be to monitor the relevant policy, and let the resulting decision about whether conditions are compliant answer the criticism. The judgment of the board should be not whether any staff action was the "right" action or not, but whether the action was based on a reasonable interpretation of, and was compliant with, the board's policy. This prevents the board from second-guessing staff decisions. It also demonstrates the board's role both in ensuring reasonable staff performance and acceptable board oversight.

What the board must avoid is yielding to the temptation to "suspend the model just this one time to deal with this extraordinary problem." There is no organizational condition or problem that Coherent Governance or Policy Governance cannot provide the means for the board to effectively deal with. That is, if the board understands how to use the tools in its toolbox!

GAME ON!

Let us make one point very clear: We have written in these last two chapters about conditions that *could,* if left unaddressed, jeopardize a board's own governing success and its efforts to forge organizational change and transformation. It is our fervent hope that your board can avoid the need to deal with any of them, but if it does encounter any of these challenges, it should feel capable of dealing with them within your policy commitments. When something such as we have identified does happen, the board must recognize the challenges for what they are: They are *potholes*; they are not *roadblocks.* Their impact will be severe only if they are left unaddressed.

Repeatedly, we have seen dedicated boards and board members confront and deal effectively with every one of these barriers and challenges in ways that are nothing short of heroic. We understand the lost momentum the board experiences when its focus is diverted to deal with them, but that sometimes is the nature of change. It doesn't come easily, but if the problems are dealt with in the proper manner, the result is worth the effort.

Your board and your organization have taken some significant steps toward creating a bold and exciting future. You will hit some potholes along the way. Don't let them deter your vision and diminish your commitment to build something bigger and better that leaves a legacy of excellent leadership and governance. Nurture what you have labored to create. As it matures, you will be amazed and proud of what you've created.

Appendix A

Monitoring Operational Expectations Policies for Compliance

(Organization)
Operational Expectations Monitoring Document
OE-8 Asset Protection

Certification of the CEO: *I certify this report to be accurate*

Signed: _____, CEO   Date: _____

_X_ In Compliance
___ Compliance with Noted Exceptions
___ Not in Compliance

Executive Summary:

Disposition of the Board: Date: _____

_X_ In Compliance
___ Compliance with Noted Exceptions
___ Not in Compliance

Appendix A

Summary statement/direction of the Board:

_____

_____

_____

_____

President: _____ CEO: _____ Date for Re-monitoring: _____

OE-8: Asset Protection	CEO		Board	
The CEO will assure that all organizational assets are adequately protected, properly maintained, appropriately used and not placed at undue risk.	In Compliance	Not in Compliance	In Compliance	Not in Compliance
CEO Interpretation: - *Organizational assets* shall mean all property and equipment that is tangible in nature with a life longer than one year owned by the Organization that cost more than $5,000. - *Adequately protected* shall mean insured for 100% replacement value. - *Properly maintained* shall mean serviced and repaired on a regular basis to retain in good operating condition. - *Appropriately used* shall mean as trained by organizational personnel in compliance with operating guidelines established by the manufacturer. - *Not placed at undue risk* shall mean safe from actions that would cause assets to be harmed or damaged or create an unsafe environment.				
Board Comments:				
OE-8.1 The CEO will maintain property and casualty insurance coverage on organizational property with limits equal to 100% of replacement value.	X			
CEO Interpretation: - *Property* shall mean facilities, vehicles, equipment, and materials with an insurable risk. - *100% of replacement value* shall mean the ability to replace and make whole property losses experienced by the organization subject to any and all deductibles.				
Indicators of Compliance - We will know we are compliant when:				

Indicators

• The organization purchases and receives the coverage declarations for property and casualty insurance equal to 100% of replacement value. Evidence of Compliance: The organization purchased and received coverage declaration for property and casualty insurance from _____ equal to 100% of replacement value subject to deductibles. Policy and coverage declarations are maintained in the Risk Management office and are available for inspection upon request.	X			
Board Comments:				
OE-8.2 The CEO will maintain both Errors and Omissions and Comprehensive General Liability insurance coverage protecting board members, staff and the organization itself in an amount that is reasonable for organizations of comparable size and character.	X			
CEO Interpretation: • *Errors and Omissions insurance* shall mean protection for board members and staff who make a mistake in performing their duties in good faith and results in harm to the organization. • *Comprehensive General Liability insurance* shall mean protection against bodily injury and property damage claims. • *Amount that is reasonable* shall mean coverage limits equal to the prevailing market standard for organizations similar to this organization, and based on recommendations of the insurance agency. • *Comparable size and character* shall mean other organizations in our general geographic area that have comparable budgets and purpose, such as _____, _____ and _____.				
Indicators of Compliance - We will know we are compliant when: • The organization has purchased and receives the coverage declarations for Errors and Omissions and Comprehensive General Liability insurance coverage. Evidence of Compliance: The organization purchased and received coverage declaration for				

Errors and Omissions and Comprehensive General Liability coverage from _____, subject to deductibles. Policy limits are $10 million per claim and aggregate for Errors and Omissions coverage, and $1 million per claim and $20 million aggregate for Comprehensive General Liability coverage. Policy and coverage declarations are maintained in the Risk Management office and are available for inspection upon request.	X	
Board Comments:		

OE-8.3 The CEO will assure that all personnel who have access to material amounts of funds are covered under the organization's general liability and crime policy.	X	
CEO Interpretation: • *All personnel* shall mean any employee of the organization. • *Material amounts* shall mean more than $500, which is equivalent to the deductible. • *General liability and crime policy* shall mean the coverage documents purchased by the organization that reimburse the organization in the event of covered loss, in this case loss resulting from an employee's illegally assuming possession of property belonging to the organization (theft).		
Indicators of Compliance - We will know we are compliant when: • The organization has purchased and receives the coverage declarations for crime coverage and the policy has been received. Evidence of Compliance: • The organization purchased and received coverage declaration for crime coverage through _____, subject to deductibles. Coverage limits for theft are $1 million per occurrence and $20 million aggregate. Policy and coverage declarations are maintained in the Risk Management office and are available for inspection upon request.	X	
Board Comments:		

OE-8.4 The CEO will protect intellectual property, information, files, records and fixed assets from loss or significant damage.	X			
CEO Interpretation: • *Intellectual property* shall mean creations of the mind: inventions, literary and artistic works, and symbols, names, images, and designs used in commerce. • *Organizational intellectual property* shall mean original materials or other documents created by employees as part of their job for use by the organization or its employees. • *Information, files and records* shall mean hard copy files and electronic data stored on organizational servers deemed critical (Finance, Human Resources, Data & Accountability) to the operations of the organization. • *Fixed assets* shall mean property and equipment with original cost of $5,000 or more. • With regard to fixed assets, *significant damage* shall mean harm or destruction requiring more than $5,000 of unplanned repair or maintenance, including labor, material, and equipment rental costs.				
Indicators of Compliance - We will know we are compliant when: • The organization receives no legal complaints that its employees have violated intellectual property rights. • Electronically stored information, files, and records are backed up each night and there is no loss of these files and records during the year, and hard copy records that are critical to the organization's mission are locked in fire-proof storage containers. • The organization repairs or replaces all fixed assets impaired by significant damage during the year. • The organization has off-site storage (servers housed in a different facility or vendor facility) or on-site fireproof safe storage of all technology data and a recovery plan for loss of information, files and records. • Intellectual property used by other organizations is used only by				

permission of the CEO.

Evidence of Compliance:

- Based on an internal review conducted by the legal office, it has been verified that the organization received no legal complaints regarding any employee violation of intellectual property rights. **X**

- Based upon an internal audit conducted by the technology department, it has been verified that the organization has received no reports of loss of critical information; files and records related to any part its operations. **X**

- The organization had significant damage to two buildings/properties during the year as a result of flooding. All damage was repaired and assets returned to original condition within 60 days of the damage. **X**

- The organization's data recovery plan for critical systems are as follows: *Infinite Operations*: Vendor is responsible for back-ups. Backups are stored at the vendor's data center in Minnesota. *Stratusphere*: Vendor is responsible for back-ups stored at vendor's data center in Phoenix. *Importdocs*: Organization is responsible for back-ups, stored on BAN (Backup Area Network) at the Administration Complex. Fourteen days of snapshots are stored off-site at a commercial electronic storage facility. *Archives (ClearVision)*: Organization is responsible for back-ups, stored at the Administration Complex. Three redundant copies made daily. Monthly copies saved locally, external hard drive and on the BAN at the Administration Complex. *JON*: went to cloud storage as of July 1, and backups are stored in vendor's data center. The CEO knows of no information critical to the organization's operation that is not adequately protected against unforeseen disaster. **X**

   All hard copy documents that are critical to the organization's mission are stored either on-site or off-site in fire-proof and locked file cabinets, as confirmed via monthly assurance reports submitted to the business office by each department head.

- The organization currently has not copyrighted any intellectual property. Intellectual property that has been developed by the organization is only shared and used by others with the permission of the CEO. **X**

Indicators

Board Comments:				
OE-8.5 The CEO may not allow facilities and equipment to be subject to improper use or insufficient maintenance.	X			
CEO Interpretation: • *Facilities and equipment* shall mean assets in excess of $5,000 original cost. • *Improper use* shall mean inappropriate operation or treatment, or utilization in a manner or for a purpose contrary to what was intended. • *Insufficient maintenance* shall mean inadequate repair, cleaning, inspection, or upkeep as recommended by manufactured specifications.				
Indicators of Compliance - We will know we are compliant when: • Internal management audits conclude that no person is injured in any of the organization's facilities or when using organization-owned equipment as a result of insufficient maintenance of the facility or equipment. • No more than five workmen's compensation claims resulting from use of equipment or insufficient facility maintenance will be filed during the year. • The Risk Management and Safety Committee verifies that no more than two improper maintenance conditions exist anywhere within the network of facilities that pose moderate or greater risk of injury to employees or customers, and that those conditions that were discovered were corrected within the shortest possible time.				
Evidence of Compliance: • There were no reports of personal injury resulting from insufficient maintenance of the facility or equipment as verified by review of monthly safety reports submitted by department heads to the Risk Management and Safety Committee. • There were two reported workmen's compensation claims as a result of use of equipment, as verified by an audit conducted by the	X			

organization's Risk Management and Safety Committee.	X		
• An internal audit revealed that one condition existed at the _____ site that, if left uncorrected, posed reasonable risk of injury to people. That condition was corrected within five working days following the audit conducted by the organization's Risk Management and Safety Committee.	X		
Board Comments:			

Authors' note: This report has been abbreviated in order to conserve space. The format and documentation presented here is intended to be applied consistently throughout the entire report.

Indicators

Appendix B

Monitoring Operational Expectations Policies for Compliance

(Organization)
Operational Expectations Monitoring Report
OE-12 Facilities

CEO Certification:

With respect to OE-12 Facilities, the CEO certifies that the information is accurate and complete, and that the District is:

__ In Compliance
__ In Compliance, with the exception of 12.10
   (as also noted in the Evidence and in the Executive Summary)
__ Not in Compliance

Signed: _____ Date: _____
                    CEO

Executive Summary:

The attached Operational Expectations Report for Facilities (OE-12) evaluates fourteen (14) sections of policy for compliance. Of the fourteen (14) policy provisions, thirteen (13) have been determined to be in compliance when evaluating identified indicators with aligned evidence, and one (1) section has been determined to not be in compliance.

The one (1) policy provision not in compliance is:

OE-12.10: "The CEO will assure that facilities are clean, safe and properly maintained."

Policy section #10 was deemed not in compliance because Indicator D, "The District completes 75 percent of all of the work orders submitted through the work order system within 60 days," failed to achieve the performance level that was projected. After analyzing the evidence, it was determined that only 70 percent of all work orders submitted (4,020 total work orders) were completed within the 60-day window. This is down from 75 percent completed within 60 days in the past year. The corrective action that has been implemented is that the Director of Maintenance and Operations will run a biweekly work order report and closely monitor completion and associated recording of completed work orders and provide direction to staff as appropriate and necessary.

DISPOSITION OF THE BOARD

With respect to OE-12 Facilities, the Board finds that the District and the Superintendent:

__ Are fully compliant
__ Are compliant with noted exception(s)

_____

_____

_____

__ Are noncompliant

Comments and Findings:

_____

_____

_____

Signed: _____ Date: _____
             Board President

(Organization)
Operational Expectations Monitoring Report
OE-12 Facilities
(Date)

The CEO shall assure that physical facilities support the accomplishments of the Board's *Results* policies, are safe and properly maintained.

INTERPRETATION

The physical facilities shall include all buildings, grounds, and infrastructure (excluding technology) throughout the District. These physical facilities shall function efficiently and effectively to provide an optimum environment for students to learn and for staff to deliver a quality program.

1. Develop and implement a five-year District Facilities Master Plan that establishes priorities for construction, renovation, and maintenance projects.	In Compliance

INTERPRETATION

The Board values effective planning for constructing, renovating, and maintaining district facilities. The plan is used as road map for all capital projects, enabling the Board to see the relationship between capital project needs and actions.

5-year District Facilities Master Plan shall mean a Facilities Master Plan, coordinated with the district computerized maintenance work order management system, that is designed to ensure that the District's school facilities support current and future education programs, and serves as a guide for assessing the need for facilities improvements and capital investments.

Priorities shall mean the ordering of needs and projects in such a way that more urgent conditions are addressed in the order of their importance.

Projects shall mean major work identified in capital budgets including the Routine Restricted Maintenance Account, Deferred Maintenance Fund, Bond Fund, Capital Facilities Fund, County School Facilities Fund, and Special Reserve Fund.

Indicators: We will know we are compliant when . . .

a. A Facilities Master Plan, that encompasses all the components represented in this policy, has been presented to the Board and contains priorities for construction, renovation, and maintenance projects.

EVIDENCE OF COMPLIANCE

a. An updated comprehensive Facilities Master Plan was presented to the Board of Education on December 12 during the Facilities Study Session. The Board was asked to provide input through May with the adoption of the new Facilities Master Plan at the June 25 meeting. *Note: At the November Facilities Study Session, the Board authorized setting aside funds to update the Facilities Master Plan. This update is nearing completion as of March 22.*

2. Identify to the Board facilities that are either unsafe or are in need of modification or reconstruction and assign highest priority to the correction of unsafe conditions.	In Compliance

INTERPRETATION

The Board values well-maintained learning environments, including facilities, for students that minimize the risk of injury to either students or staff. The board expects staff to routinely analyze and assess the condition of district facilities to determine if they meet Board values. Where conditions do not meet Board values, staff is expected to provide to the Board a list of conditions that either are unsafe or are in need of modification or renovation, as well as a prioritized plan for removing unsafe conditions and for bringing facilities up to standard.

Unsafe condition shall mean a condition that does not meet an applicable code or generally accepted industry standard or a condition that can reasonably be expected to pose risk of physical harm to students or staff.

Indicators: We will know we are compliant when . . .

a. A list of facilities conditions that have been identified as unsafe, are in poor repair, or are in need of modification or renovation is compiled and presented to the board.

EVIDENCE OF COMPLIANCE

a. The Board was provided at its January meeting a list of facilities that have been identified as being in a state of unacceptable repair or were in need of modification or renovation. The report included a priority list of conditions that were deemed unsafe, all of which had been corrected by staff. That report is appended to this monitoring report. A table showing related work orders, including a sample of a Facilities Inspection Tool (FIT), are provided in the Appendix under Sub Policy #2a.

3.	Create and update a yearly preventive maintenance plan.	In Compliance

INTERPRETATION

The Board expects staff to routinely assess the needs of district facilities and to effectively allocate available resources to ensure that they are maintained to the highest possible level in order to maximize their lifespan.

Preventive Maintenance Plan shall mean a plan that outlines all of the maintenance work necessary to mitigate the potential loss of use of any facilities or equipment and to help limit or reduce the cost of major repairs.

Indicators: We will know we are compliant when . . .

a. A complete Facilities and Equipment Preventive Maintenance Plan, complete with appropriate timelines and action steps that map current and planned maintenance and repair of District facilities and equipment, is formally presented to the board for its information.

EVIDENCE OF COMPLIANCE

a. The required Facilities and Equipment preventive Maintenance Plan is appended to this report as evidence of compliance. (*Appendix* under Sub Policy #3.)

Author's note: This report is abbreviated to save space. The single noncompliant section, Section 10, is shown as follows:

10.	Ensure that facilities are clean, safe, and properly maintained.	Not in Compliance

INTERPRETATION

The Board expects that facilities will be free from dirt and trash, will be orderly, and will be maintained in such a way that the physical well-being of students and staff is reasonably ensured and that the basic purpose of the buildings is fulfilled.

Clean shall mean relatively free of trash (except in approved receptacles) and dirt and conforming to applicable health department standards.

Safe shall mean free from physical conditions or dangers that pose risk to the well-being of students, staff, and stakeholders.

Properly maintained shall mean facilities will be kept in a condition that they may be continuously utilized for their intended purpose.

Indicators: We will know we are compliant when . . .

a. The district passes all required annual inspections and construction inspections in accordance with applicable federal, state, county, and local codes.
b. Inspection data from the State's Facility Inspection Tool (FIT) administered by County Office of Education personnel report that all sites evaluated meet or exceed expected cleanliness and safety levels (a rating of "Fair" or higher).
c. Principal surveys reveal that 80 percent of all principals rate O and M performance related to their schools to be acceptable or exceptional, and that any specific issues are addressed in a manner acceptable to the principals.
d. Internal tracking systems conclude the District completes 75 percent of all of the work orders submitted through the work order system within 60 days.

EVIDENCE OF COMPLIANCE

a. The Facility Inspection Tool (FIT) guidebook developed by the Office of Public School Construction (OPSC) is used for the self-assessment of district facilities. During the last fiscal year ending June 30, staff inspected all school sites and identified the condition of eight (8) district schools as "good" and seven (7) as "exemplary." In addition, ten (10) schools inspected by County Office of Education were given a rating of "Exemplary" and three (3) as "Fair."
b. All Facilities Inspection Tools (FIT) provided to the Assistant Superintendent of Business Services by the Director of Maintenance and Operations

for the most recent school year validate that all district schools met or exceeded expectations for cleanliness.
c. Principal survey results indicate that 84 percent of all principals consider the maintenance and operations provided to their schools to be either acceptable or exceptional. See 2016–2017 "Customer Service Satisfaction Survey Results" in the Appendix under Sub Policy #10.
d. For the last school year, the District completed 70 percent of all of work orders submitted through the work order system within 60 days. The performance target was 75 percent.

Appendix C

Monitoring Results for Reasonable Progress

Sample One: Interpretation and Indicators Report
(Organization Name)
Results Monitoring Document R-2: Quality of Life

Certification of the CEO: I certify this report to be accurate:

Signed: _____, CEO   Date:_____

_X_ Request Approval of Interpretation/Indicators

EXECUTIVE SUMMARY

In preparation for formal monitoring, the CEO offers this interpretation of the board's stated values in R.2. We have included, for your information, Appendix 1: "Strategic Direction," which overviews some of the strategic choices the CEO and staff are making in pursuit of the board's expected outcomes as we move toward formal monitoring within the year.

SUMMATIVE ANALYSIS: N/A

DISPOSITION OF THE BOARD

_X_ Approval of Interpretation/Indicators as Reasonable
___ Approval Denied

Summary Statement/Motion of the Board

The Board finds the CEO's interpretation, choice of indicators, and future performance targets to be reasonable. The interpretation assures us that the Board's intent and values about the quality of life we wish for our elders is understood and will be strategically sought by the CEO and staff. Additionally, we find the CEO's choice of indicators and future targets to be reasonable. The board recognizes that targets will evolve over time as data are collected. The Board finds the CEO's interpretation, choice of indicators, and future performance targets to be reasonable.

Signed: _____, President

Date: _____ Re-monitor: _____

R-2: Our elderly will maintain the highest possible quality of life, including physical and mental health and wellness.

REASONABLE INTERPRETATION

I interpret this policy to mean that the Board values that our elders, as they age, will be served in a manner that permits them to maintain the highest level of independence and personal enjoyment of life possible.

- *Elders:* Defined as all individuals who are eligible to receive the organization's services and who have elected to participate in our current and future programs and services.
- *The highest quality of life*: Elders will enjoy a lifestyle, to the extent possible, to which they are accustomed and that supports their personal goals, life choice, dignity, and respect in a safe, enriching, and homelike environment. Elders will have meaningful and consistent relationships with family, friends, social groups, and community; enjoy and practice their cultural traditions, language, food choices, values, and spirituality; enjoy a diversity of activities in their areas of interest; and continue to have access to and a place in the broader community and world.
- *Physical health and wellness*: Elders will enjoy, to the extent possible, their fullest potential of mobility and appearance while pain and illness are mitigated to support their independence, self-worth, and quality of life.
- *Mental health and wellness:* Elders will enjoy, to the extent possible, the highest level of emotional and cognitive well-being and exercise their intellect and interests while any behavioral illnesses are mitigated to the extent possible to support their independence, self-worth, and quality of life.

INDICATORS

Utilizing current and future clinical systems and mechanisms (Quality Assurance Meetings), measures (e.g., MDS, QIS/State Surveys, Quality Indicators/ADLs) and utilizing experts (state and consultants) to create a platform to continuously evaluate and upgrade services:

- 75 percent of our elderly will respond to our "Customer Satisfaction Surveys" that they feel they are able to maintain their highest possible quality of life, including physical and mental health and wellness via or in part by our programs and services.
- 75 percent of our elderly family members will respond to our "Customer Satisfaction Survey" that their loved one is able maintain the highest possible quality of life, including physical and mental health and wellness via or in part by our programs and services.

APPENDIX 1—STRATEGIC DIRECTION (FOR BOARD INFORMATION ONLY)

We will accomplish these outcomes through our strategic efforts of:

- Committing to a resident- and participant-centered and -directed approach.
- Creating goals, objectives, standards of operations, systems, and measures reflective of a "premier" organization that honors and respects our elderly.
- Proactively enhancing and expanding current programs and services through identification of "best practices" and trends. Ongoing educational efforts to our entire community including Health Care Conferences, online resources, and one-on-one consultations.
- Ensuring we engage high-quality staff and business partners (vendors) and actively involve volunteers and family members in support of our elderly by providing appropriate resources and trainings.
- Maintaining compliance to all laws and regulations including "Resident's Rights."
- Creating a strategic plan that supports meeting the needs of our evolving elderly community.
- Developing and implementing an overall budget and allocating appropriate resources to support the organizational and our elderly goals, objectives, and culture.

Appendix D

Results Monitoring Report

Sample Two: Monitoring Results for Reasonable Progress
(Organization)
Results Monitoring Report R-2.3: Use of Technology

Superintendent Certification: I certify this report to be accurate:

Signed: _____ Date: _____
           Superintendent

With respect to Results Policy R-2.3: "Use of technology to gain, analyze, evaluate, and present information," the Superintendent certifies that the information is accurate and complete and that the District is:

__ Making Reasonable Progress
X Making Reasonable Progress with noted exception(s):
    While students in fifth and eighth grades in the advanced level met the 5 percent target for one year's growth, students in the proficient level in both grades regressed.
__ Failing to make Reasonable Progress

EXECUTIVE SUMMARY: COMBINING ADVANCED AND PROFICIENT LEVELS

At the end of the previous year, 72 percent of eighth graders were proficient or advanced on NETS-S as compared to the prior four successive years: 71 percent, 53 percent, 48 percent, and 42 percent. The current level of proficiency represents an increase of 24 percent in the proficient and advanced ranges over the last three years. As well, 64 percent of fifth graders were proficient or advanced on NETS-S as compared to 50 percent in the prior school year, representing an increase of 14 percent in the proficient and advanced ranges over the prior year.

DISPOSITION OF THE BOARD

With respect to Results Policy R-2.3, "Use of technology to gain, analyze, evaluate, and present information," the Board finds that the District and the Superintendent are:

__ Making Reasonable Progress
X Making Reasonable Progress with noted exception(s)
__ Failing to make Reasonable Progress

SUMMARY STATEMENT AND VOTE OF THE BOARD

While the targets for 5 percent growth in the combined advanced/proficient were not met in both grades for this academic year, the Board commends the Superintendent for the trajectory of growth and performance over the past eight years. It is clear that students in our system are advancing in their technology skills. The strategies you have employed are working. The Board-approved targets for separate levels versus the way the data are presented in the Executive Summary is confusing. We need to review the recommended targets and reporting requirements prior to board approval of targets for the next cycle.

Signed: _____ Date: _____
               Board President

PURPOSE

The purpose of this Results Monitoring Report is to provide the Board with appropriate data demonstrating student progress in the use of technology for creativity and self-expression and to gain, analyze, and evaluate information.

CRITERIA TO DETERMINE REASONABLE PROGRESS

- The Results policy has been reasonably interpreted.
- Appropriate indicators have been selected that accurately measure student achievement.
- The data is sufficient to allow the Board to decide.
- Students show performance improvement over time, measured against performance targets.

R-2.3 Students will:

Use technology to gain, analyze, evaluate, and present information.

INTERPRETATION

Students will demonstrate research and information fluency, critical thinking, problem solving and decision-making, digital citizenship, and an understanding of technology operations and concepts and communication and collaboration. Students will:

- "Gain information": demonstrate skills in accessing knowledge, material, and content
- "Analyze information": demonstrate skills in evaluating the reliability and validity of electronically sourced information
- "Evaluate information": assess the quality of information and determine if the information is reliable, valid, and useful
- "Present information": demonstrate and display learning through the creative and critical use of technology

DEFINITION OF TERMS

1. National Educational Technology Standards for Students (NETS-S)
    The current NETS-S was developed by the International Society for Technology in Education in 2007. In the absence of state standards for technology, the NETS-S is incorporated into the District's 2013–2016

Educational Technology Plan and used as a principal indicator. There are twenty standards distributed across the following six categories:

- *Creativity and Innovation:* Students demonstrate creative thinking, construct knowledge, and develop innovative products and processes using technology.
- *Communication and Collaboration:* Students use digital media and environments to communicate and work collaboratively, including at a distance, to support individual learning and contribute to the learning of others.
- *Research and Information Fluency:* Students apply digital tools to gather, evaluate, and use information.
- *Critical Thinking, Problem Solving, and Decision Making:* Students use critical thinking skills to plan and conduct research, manage projects, solve problems, and make informed decisions using appropriate digital tools and resources.
- *Digital Citizenship:* Students understand human, cultural, and societal issues related to technology and practice legal and ethical behavior.
- *Technology Operations and Concepts:* Students demonstrate a sound understanding of technology concepts, systems, and operations.

2. Simple Assessment

   SimpleAssessment from InfoSource Learning is an individualized assessment of all NETS-S proficiency levels. Teachers and administrators collaborated to create a district-specific assessment utilizing items from SimpleAssessment.

3. Student Proficiency Levels

   Student proficiency levels were defined based on previously released proficiency level ranges from the State Department of Education: 86 percent of the questions must be answered correctly to receive an advanced score.

INDICATORS

The District's Student Tech Assessment was administered to all eighth-grade students at all middle schools. Data from 2010, 2011, and 2012 represents the results of the Simple Assessment, 2013 through 2017, and is from the revised Student Tech Assessment. At the Board's request, a technology assessment was also administered to fifth-grade students in 2016 and again in 2017.

TARGET

A target of 5 percent growth of advanced students and a 5 percent cumulative growth of the combined proficient and advanced will be met.

Indicators	Grade	Target	Results
District Tech Assessment	8	5% growth	Advanced Met
			Advanced/Proficient Not Met
District Tech Assessment	5	5% growth	Advanced Met
			Advanced/Proficient Not Met

INDICATOR NETS-S ASSESSMENT DATA

Grade 8 NETS-S Proficiency Levels: Last eight years

Year	Baseline	Two	Three	Four	Five	Six	Seven	Eight
Advanced	1%	8%	8%	17%	21%	25%	42%	47%
Proficient	11%	30%	29%	25%	27%	28%	29%	25%
Basic	28%	31%	27%	27%	32%	22%	19%	16%
Below Basic	27%	21%	21%	18%	15%	20%	7%	10%
Far Below Basic	33%	10%	15%	13%	5%	5%	3%	2%

Grade 5 NETS-S Proficiency Levels: Year One Baseline

Year	Baseline	Two
Advanced	18%	35%
Proficient	32%	29%
Basic	30%	28%
Below Basic	18%	7%
Far Below Basic	2%	1%

DATA SUMMARY—WHAT THE DATA TELLS US

It is clear that student technology skills have increased significantly over time. While the growth in advanced/proficient only increased by 1 percent over the previous year, the percentage of students in the advanced range has increased over the last eight years.

In addition to increasing the number and percentage of students who are proficient or advanced, it is also extremely encouraging to see that students demonstrating the lowest level of proficiency (Far Below Basic) has decreased to only 2 percent. This is evidence that we are working to effectively close the technology access gap in all of our schools and communities.

The growth made by our current fifth-grade students is also extremely encouraging, with 64 percent of the students at the proficient or advanced level, which is again an indicator of the power of the districtwide 1:1 initiative, which starts officially in grade three.

We believe the increased student performance is based on several significant factors:

- Student access to devices and Internet through both school-based and home-based programs. (While schools for several years have had sufficient numbers of devices and Internet bandwidth, the last two years have seen a substantial increase in the number of students who are taking their Chromebooks home each day, keeping them over the weekend, or in many instances keeping them at home altogether. When students don't have access to Internet at home, the district has provided take-home Wi-Fi Internet "hot spots." The addition of these devices has helped to move computer-based targeted practice, research, and document/presentation to the home.)
- Increased professional development for teachers has also positively impacted the outcomes of students taking the Technology Assessment. All 1 to 1 teachers have participated in a minimum of three days of training with regular coaching and support to help them to utilize the devices and align their instruction so that technology skills are embedded and developed during the delivery of day-to-day core content instruction.
- The Technology team regularly works with teachers and curriculum experts. Teachers are connected to the Technology standards through the units of study and other curriculum shared by the district.

APPENDIX: STRATEGIC DIRECTION—
FOR BOARD INFORMATION ONLY

Students' access to technology has rapidly evolved over the last five years since the start of the third through twelfth grade 1:1 pilot. The following educational technology advancements that support student access have been achieved:

- Four years ago, ETIS established Google Apps for Education (GAFE) pilot and teacher pilot of Google Classroom
  - Full adoption of GAFE and Google Classroom
  - 4.2 million Google Documents created since 2011

- Creation of ChromeWarrior and cyber champions, which are gamified, *technology-focused* professional development platforms (Model of Academic Excellence Winner)
- Extensive teacher and office staff professional development, including:
  - Google Applications for Education (GAFE)
  - Google Classroom
  - iPad and Chromebook 1:1 trainings
  - Extending the learning day strategies (Blended and Flipped Solutions)
  - Establishing web presence
  - Advanced GAFE

- Digital Citizenship Strategies
  - Classroom management in a 1:1 environment

- 24/7 Program (1:1 Take home)
- Completed 1:1 device to students from grades 3 through 12
- CakeWalk coding club pilots at four schools
- T-Mobile HotSpot pilot (all 24/7 sites and IEP support at two sites)
- Broadband access to students

Additional infrastructure and support strategies have been deployed in the past three years to include the following:

- Wireless controller–based technologies
- Upgraded fiber and networking equipment
- Advanced Internet filtering solutions
- Online safety monitoring and alerting
- Customized grade-level professional development, in-class coaching, on-demand professional development, and fast deployment support

FOR A SEPARATE VOTE: REQUEST FOR BOARD APPROVAL OF NEW TARGETS

Students scoring Advanced and Advanced/Proficient will each increase by 5 percent over the prior year.

Appendix E

Engagement with Stakeholders

SAMPLE 1—SETTING UP KEY COMMUNICATORS

Author's Note: Key Communicators is a simple idea and really quite easy to get up and running. Individual members of the board identify persons they consider to be opinion leaders, share their lists, and identify as a board twenty-five to thirty individuals they agree shape opinion in the community of owners.

KEY COMMUNICATORS: A GUIDELINE FOR GETTING STARTED

Reference: GC-3–board work to link with owners and clients

Purpose: Accessing the Grapevine

1. A network of influential people designated to maintain continuing two-way communication with the board.
2. An opportunity for the board to provide timely, full, and firsthand information about the organization to influential people who, in turn, can share their information with those with whom they interact.
3. An opportunity for the board to receive information, insight, and counsel from the "community grapevine."

Identification of Opinion Leaders

These are twenty-five to thirty people identified by the board, people others listen to when they talk about your industry.

Preparing for the First Meeting

1. Establish: date, time, place, topics
2. Board members divide the list and personally contact suggested participants by phone, sending a follow-up postcard with confirmation of the details of the meeting.
3. Provide refreshments and name tags.
4. Use roundtable seating.
5. Board greets and sits with invitees.

Postcard or Email Confirmation Copy (send after phone contact):

> Thank you for agreeing to be a Key Communicator partnering with our board. We look forward to building continuing communication relationships with you and the other identified opinion leaders for the next year. Our hope is that you will provide your insight, information, and wisdom about matters of mutual concern. In return, we will provide you full and timely information about significant board and organizational issues and concerns.
>
> Meeting logistics: Building and street address
Date and time:
We will begin and end on time!
Contact to confirm: Board Secretary, (name and phone)

Agenda

7:00 a.m.: Welcome and introductions (*One board member comfortable with public speaking leads the meeting. You may rotate the role among board members from meeting to meeting. Remember, this is board work, not staff. Arrange for members to record answers on flipcharts at appropriate discussion points.*)

7:30: Explain purpose of Key Communicators.

> The board has recognized the need to develop stronger connections to the owners it serves. Key Communicators is a tool that has been chosen because of its success with boards across the country.
>
> Each of you has been identified by board members as people who are listened to when you speak. We consider you to be opinion leaders who are sought out by others for more intimate knowledge about our organization.
>
> Our purpose is twofold: to provide you with full and complete information, and provide a forum for deeper discussion about issues we are grappling with.

The second purpose is to ask you to share your insights with us about topics of concern to the board and to contact us as you hear things in the community about the organization. Let us help you respond to rumors, to inaccuracies, and to emerging issues.

7:40: Provide a quick update on current issues (sample issues)

- Board reorganization
- Good news on organizational results
- New end result

8:05: Identify issues members want to hear about and discuss at upcoming meetings

8:10: Ask participants:

1. Will you meet with us on a regular basis? Monthly? Bi-monthly? Quarterly?
2. Preferred length of meeting? Preferred Location? Time of day?
3. Will you agree to receive emails or phone calls as issues or events occur to get full, timely, and accurate information?
4. Will you agree to contact us with information or to ask for information? (Give them a voice mail and email contact.)

8:30: Adjourn, confirming the next meeting as your final piece of business.

Appendix F

Engagement Plan to Further Define Results

SAMPLE 2—DISTRICT ENGAGEMENT PLAN

Author's Note: This example is from a large school district that used this well-designed approach to share the board's first draft of a Citizenship Result, to solicit feedback, and eventually, to gain support for district efforts. We have provided the initial draft of the Result policy and the protocol. After the campaign, the board revised the Result policy reflecting what members heard. This was the "guide" for members to use as they conducted the group conversations.

R-3

Policy Type: Results

Citizenship (draft)

All students will be responsible citizens and productive participants in their communities.

3.1. Students will demonstrate knowledge of their community, its history and its global context.
3.2. Students will appreciate what they have.

Focus Group Protocol

Introduction (7:30 p.m.–7:31 p.m.):
    Introduce yourself. Explain your role as a facilitator and their role as a participant. Emphasize that your role is to pose the questions, ensure that

everyone has a chance to respond, and record their responses *(remember to write their responses VERBATIM on the flipcharts)*. Stress that we want their ideas and believe that they have the information we need to accomplish our task.

Purpose (7:31 p.m.–7:35 p.m.): The purpose of the focus group session is to:

- Gain insight into how community members define student citizenship,
- Identify citizenship behaviors you expect our students to demonstrate, and
- Offer suggestions about how we should measure whether students are good citizens or not.

Review the draft Citizenship Result policy.

Process (7:35 p.m.–7:36 p.m.):
Explain that you will pose the question and give them some time (about 30 seconds) to jot down a few ideas. Position up front to ensure that everyone has a chance to answer you. Plan to call upon participants for the answers (explain how you will do this). Also, let them know that it's okay to "pass" once when called upon. If people do pass, be sure to go back and collect their response.

Question 1 (Context setting—frame of reference) (7:36 p.m.–7:46 p.m.):
When you think about being an American citizen today and in the future, how do you define citizenship for yourself? What are some of the values, traits, and characteristics of a model American citizen?
After they have exhausted their responses, ask:
Now let's think about an American citizen in our county, specifically, a School District student. Are there other values, traits, and characteristics that you would add to your lists?

Question 2 (Demonstrated behaviors) (7:46 p.m.–7:56 p.m.):
Looking at the list you've just generated, what behaviors or activities would a student need to demonstrate to show others that they are model or good American citizens?
After they have exhausted their responses, ask:
Do they need to do anything else to show they are good American citizens?

Question 3 (Measurements) (7:56 p.m.–8:06 p.m.):
Now consider all of your responses and think about the following question. If we want to know about student academic achievement, we usually look at test scores and other important measurements. If we want to report to you about student progress and accomplishment of good or model citizenship, what types of information or measurements could we use?

Closing Remarks (8:06 p.m.):

Thank them for their participation. Explain that we will be conducting sessions just like this one in two other clusters. We plan to collect all of the data, analyze their responses, and look for trends, similarities, and differences in communities' expectations. A report will be made available to them when the process is completed. Invite them to stay for the next step of the Engagement Meeting and join everyone back in the cafeteria.

Appendix G

Board Listening Campaign

Author's Note: This campaign is textbook-perfect for public boards that want to proactively engage their community of owners and engender support. It worked!

MISSION

Focus on the supporters, the semi-supporters and the uninformed. *Do not* waste time and energy on the naysayers. Word of mouth is the most powerful and impactful means to communicate.

GOAL

To provide opportunities for two-way conversation with the owners about current board and district challenges and to build understanding based on factual information.

OUTPUT OBJECTIVE

1. Inform the public about district initiatives and attributes and ask for feedback and input;
2. Confront and correct misinformation and rumors;
3. Gain support for district initiatives through various channels on communications and face-to-face communications to external and internal audiences.

IMPACT OBJECTIVES

1. By May 31, 75 percent of the public feel they are informed and heard by the board and are supportive of district initiatives and the direction of the board, as measured through simple, random phone surveys throughout the summer or given by their child's teacher.
2. By May 31, 80 percent of the staff feel they are informed and heard by the board and are supportive of district initiatives and the direction of the board, as measured through district climate survey.

TARGET AUDIENCE: SUPPORTERS, THE SEMI-SUPPORTERS, AND THE UNINFORMED

- Staff
- Parents
- Community partnerships

STRATEGIES

1. Focus on a push strategy of communications where board members are *going to* staff and patrons to connect with them.
2. Use district channels of communication such as the ___, ___ and ___.
3. Measure community opinion and evaluate plan based on pre-measurement of community (May) opinion telephone survey, (October) mid-plan measurement and post-plan measurement (May). Cost: Estimated $30,000.

INTERNAL COMMUNICATION TACTICS

1. Weekly communication message to staff connected to the ___
   - Message from the board: a message from a different board member each week
   - Address positive and negative issues going on
   - We will "Stay the Course" and continue our duties and expectations
   - Thank you for your hard work
2. Continue the "Unsung Heroes" of our school district program.
3. Have one board member attend one staff meeting at each school for a Q&A discussion about allegations and issues going on in the district.

4. Develop a speaker's bureau of teachers who support the district's initiatives. Utilize this speaker's bureau to communicate to the public and internal staff groups.

EXTERNAL COMMUNICATION TACTICS

1. Connect with parent support groups like the PTO, and parent volunteers to host coffees.
2. Schedule one coffee hosted by small groups of patrons where board members attend to complete the three components of the goal.
3. Create a group of patrons who are willing to sign their name to letters to the editor for the purpose of completing the three components of the goal. One to three letters to the editor should be published in the local newspaper per week.
4. Board members go to the community to complete the components of the goal through:
   - Afterschool care locations when parents are picking up their kids
   - School events such as concerts, literacy nights, parent-teacher conferences and back-to-school nights
5. Continue to infiltrate media channels and send press releases to the media regarding board meeting dates, agenda/discussion items, district initiatives, and events where board members are talking to the community.
6. Design a fold-out business card–size marketing piece to hand out for the board that states the main goals and mission of the board and contact information.
7. Attend events related to community organizations such as community centers and other communal places.

COMMUNICATION DEPARTMENT ROLE

- Design and distribution
- Keep an ongoing calendar of events for the board to attend of internal and external meetings
- Update public opinion dashboard—lessons learned, talking points, main questions/concerns, updates on naysayer communication, telephone survey statistics, schools visited, group discussions, media articles, opinion letters, etc.
- Manage the telephone survey program

- Manage talking points to the community
- Manage media inquiries
- Assign engagements for speaker's bureau
- Research speaking opportunities
- Track stakeholders, parent groups and PTO liaisons in the district
- Maintain social media channels

ADDITIONAL BUDGET NEEDED

Telephone Survey $30,000
  (Can be justified to community because we want to get community input and figure out where to go from here.)

Board marketing handout $4,000

Additional radio advertising $15,000
  (Can be justified to community because we want to attract more students and families for more government funding.)

Appendix H

Agendas for Good Governance

SAMPLE ONE: BOARD OF EDUCATION AGENDA

Date and Location:

1. Convene—5:00 p.m.
   a. Call to Order and Roll Call
   b. Pledge of Allegiance: led by a student from the __ School.
   c. Mission Statement: read by a student from the __ School.

2. GC.2   Adopt agenda—5:05 p.m.

3. R.1   Showcasing Schools—5:10 p.m.

Students will make reasonable progress toward one year's academic gain each year, with low achieving students progressing more quickly, in the following disciplines: Reading, Writing, Math, and Science.

   a. The Opportunity School/Challenger Program
   b. Principal's Report: Presented by _____

4. GC-3, BSR-5   Focus on Results—5:25 p.m.

   R.2—Monitoring Report on Achievement: Literacy

5. Focus on Operational Performance—6:05 p.m.

   OE-12- Facilities Monitoring Report

5. GC-6, GC-6.d   Board Development—6:20 p.m.

The Board will follow an annual work plan that includes continual monitoring and review of all policies, dialog sessions with community and staff groups, and activities to improve Board performance.

    a. Association of School Boards Fall Regional Meeting Report
    b. Association of School Boards Delegate Assembly Report

6. GC-3.3   Public Comment—6:30 p.m.

Initiate and maintain constructive two-way dialogue with students, staff, parents and citizens as a means to engage all stakeholders in the work of the Board and the District.

7. GC-3   Monitoring Board Performance—6:45 p.m.

The Board will monitor its own performance

    a. GC-6E   Review Annual Work Plan

The Board will follow an annual work plan that includes continual monitoring and review of all policies, dialog sessions with community and staff groups, and activities to improve Board performance.

    b. GC-6.2c   Review Monitoring Schedule

Scheduled monitoring of all policies.

8. GC-2.4   Superintendent's Consent Agenda—6:55 p.m.

All administrative matters delegated to the Superintendent that are required to be approved by the Board will be acted upon by the Board via the consent agenda.

    a. Personnel Employment
    b. Financial Statement

9. GC-2.4   Board Consent Agenda—7:00 p.m.

The Board will use a consent agenda as a means to expedite the disposition of routine matters and dispose of other items of business it chooses not to discuss.

    a. Approval of Minutes from September 7 and September 23.

Recess (5 minutes)

10. GC-2.2   Board Debrief of Meeting—7:10 p.m.

The Board will assess the quality of each meeting by debriefing following its conclusion.

11. Adjourn—7:20 p.m.

Appendix I

Typical Agenda Outline for Public Board

Author's note: This is a standard agenda format used by many public boards that is consistent with the work outlined in GC-3, the board's job description.

Board of Education Meeting
AGENDA

1. Convene 6:30 p.m.
   Call to order, roll call, establish quorum, Pledge of Allegiance

2. Adopt agenda: 6:31 p.m.

3. Public Comment: 6:33 p.m.   GC-3
   Members of the public who desire to address the board on any topic related to board work are welcome to do so at this time. Speakers are requested to limit their remarks to not more than 3 minutes; to appoint a spokesperson if the concern is a group concern, and to supplement verbal presentations with written reports, if necessary or desired.

4. Superintendent Consent Agenda
   (legally required) 6:45 p.m.   BCR-3, GC-2.6

   a. Personnel appointments
   b. Approve award of contracts
   c. Approve textbooks

5. Board Consent Agenda 6:50 p.m.   GC-2.6

   a. Approve minutes

6. Matters Reserved for Board Action 6:55 p.m.

   a. Approve change orders for new construction projects   GC-1
   b. Approve appointment of financial auditor

7. Focus on Results 7:15 p.m.   GC-3.5

   a. Character and Citizenship Monitoring Report   R-4
   b. Indicators and Baseline (Internal Report from Superintendent)

8. Focus on Operational Performance 8:00 p.m.   GC-3.5

   a. Learning Environment/Treatment of Students Monitoring Report   OE-18

9. Board Development 8:15 p.m.   GC-3.3
   Instructive conversation with the district's curriculum staff and guest experts about academic standards and assessments and their application to board Policy

10. Board debriefing of this evening's meeting 8:45 p.m.   GC-2.3

11. Adjourn 8:55 p.m.

Glossary

Baseline: current performance measure that serves as the base against which future progress will be measured.

Benchmark: comparison of one organization's performance against other comparable organizations.

CEO: Chief Executive Officer, Superintendent, Executive Director, Chief Superintendent, president—the board's sole link with the operational organization.

Clients: those persons who are served by your organization; those who receive the benefit of what you do—those whom you exist to serve.

Compliance: operating in a manner that achieves the *gold standards* identified by your board in the Operational Expectations policies.

Data: subjective and objective information, statistics, facts, figures, records gathered to document compliance with Executive Limitations or Operational Expectations policies and reasonable progress toward Results or Ends policies.

Formative: information intended to be used for internal, ongoing improvement as opposed to summative judgment.

Governance: the role of a board of directors in its exercise of power and authority over an organization.

Governing Policy: written values identified by the board to govern four areas:

- *Governance Culture or Governance Process:* values by which the board will self-govern;
- *Board/CEO Relationship or Governance Management Connection:* values by which the board will relate to the CEO, defining delegation of authority and means for establishing CEO and organizational accountability;

- *Operational Expectations or Executive Limitations:* values that establish the standards for the organization's performance, including actions and conditions the board expects to exist and those to be avoided as the CEO makes operational decisions to achieve organizational outcomes; and
- *Results or Ends:* outcomes to be achieved for and by clients.

Indicators: the measures, assessments, surveys, and data points that will be used to judge organizational performance.

Longitudinal: progress over time.

Monitoring: a process that establishes the current state of organizational performance. Operational Expectations monitoring reports document the state of compliance with Operational Expectations policies. Results monitoring reports establish whether reasonable progress has been made toward achieving Results.

Noncompliance: failure to create operational conditions that meet the board's standards.

Organization: any entity created to fulfill owners' needs.

Owners: those whose support is necessary for the organization to survive; individuals whose lives are benefited, either directly or indirectly, by what the organization does.

Policy: the shared value of a board majority that drives action.

Preamble: the largest value statement of any policy; the opening statement. All other subparts of a policy are smaller values related to the larger preamble statement.

Reasonable interpretation: statements intended to assure the board that the CEO understands the values represented by the board's policy statement and can apply that interpretation to organizational performance.

Reasonable person: a reasonable person is appropriately informed, capable, aware of the law, and fair-minded such that he is able to render a fair and unbiased decision.

Reasonable Progress: organizational performance over time that represents improvement from one point in time to another toward achieving the Results defined by the board. The board, using the "reasonable person standard," according to approved indicators and performance targets developed by the CEO, ultimately defines reasonable progress.

Stakeholders: all individuals and groups of people who are, or might be, affected by the organization's performance. Those who hold a stake in what the organization does.

Summative: the summation of, or conclusions reached about, prior monitoring of organizational performance.

Target: a measure of future or predicted performance forecast for each approved indicator.

About the Authors

Linda J. Dawson has more than thirty-five years of experience as a skilled author, consultant, coach, and facilitator with a career in teaching and administration, agency public relations, and association leadership. As an executive with the Colorado Association of School Boards, she developed cutting-edge governance training programs, which were widely regarded at the national level. The ensuing demand for her services in other states led to her decision to cofound AGI Aspen Group International, LLC in 1993.

Linda attended Westmont College in Santa Barbara and graduated from Rockford University in Illinois. She was project director of a three-year project for the National School Boards Foundation on data-based decision-making for boards. She is in demand as a consultant, speaker, trainer, and facilitator, both nationally and internationally. Linda is a widely published author in trade and association magazines. She is an accredited public relations professional (APR), a qualified Myers-Briggs Type Indicator consultant, and certified in strategic planning and trained by Dr. John Carver in his model of Policy Governance.

Dr. Randy Quinn served for thirty years as executive director of two state school boards associations, in Alabama for nineteen years and in Colorado for eleven years, before making a full-time commitment to AGI in 1999. He has written more than four hundred articles for publication in various journals, and has served on the boards of directors of numerous state and national organizations. He cofounded AGI Aspen Group International in 1993 with Linda to extend his work throughout the United States and internationally.

Randy earned his undergraduate degree from Jacksonville State University in Alabama, and his MA and EdD degrees from the University of Alabama.

He, too, is a certified strategic planner and a graduate of John Carver's Policy Governance Academy.

Together, Dawson and Quinn have published and coauthored innumerable articles and authored two previous books also published by Rowman & Littlefield, *Good Governance Is a Choice* and *Boards That Matter*. Additionally, they are responsible for the development and distribution of board training materials used internationally through the International School Services in Princeton, New Jersey.

AGI Aspen Group International LLC serves governing boards of all types, principally public and nonprofit boards. Aspen's special area of focus is public school boards, primarily due to the world from which both Linda and Randy came. The company also works with a range of other types of public and nonprofit boards, including cities, counties, self-insurance pools, health care organizations, conservation districts, elder care organizations, and others.

Since forming AGI in 1993, Linda and Randy have consulted with boards in most of the fifty states and others on three continents, including boards in Morocco, Korea, Borneo, Mexico, Singapore, and Canada.

Their work with boards "on the ground and in the trenches" led them to develop their own governing model variation in 2005. That course of action was taken primarily as a means to meet the specific needs of public boards, whose members face demands and pressures with which members of many other types of boards are unfamiliar.

Their governing model, Coherent Governance, is described in their first book, *Good Governance Is a Choice*.

www.ingramcontent.com/pod-product-compliance
Lightning Source LLC
Chambersburg PA
CBHW021849300426
44115CB00005B/84